MIHAI EMINESCU
POEMS

EXECUTIVE BOARD
129th Session RARIS, 6 Iune 1988

great anniversaries

„Commemoration of the centenary of the death of the Roumanian national poet Mihai Eminescu"

MIHAI EMINESCU
POEMS

English version
by
CORNELIU M. POPESCU

EDITURA CARTEA ROMÂNEASCĂ

1989

Cover by GH. BALTOC

ISBN 973-23-0082-5

The vignet tes were taken from Mihai Eminescu, Poezii, second
Maiorescu edition, Bucharest, 1885.

PREFAȚA LA EDIȚIA D'INTÂI

Colecția de față cuprinde toate poesiile lui Eminescu publicate în « Convorbiri Literare » de vre-o doisprezece ani încoace, precum și cele aflate pănă acum numai în manuscript pe la unele persoane particulare.

Publicarea se face în lipsa poetului din țară. El a fost totdeauna prea impersonal și prea nepăsător de soarta lucrărilor sale, pentru a fi putut fi înduplecat să se îngrijească însuș de o asemenea culegere, cu toată stăruința amicilor săi literari.

Poesiile, așa cum se presintă în paginile următoare, nu sunt dar revăzute de Eminescu și sunt prin urmare lipsite de îndreptările ce avea de gînd să le facă, cel puțin la cele vechi (Venere și Madonă, Mortua est, Egipetul, Noaptea, Ânger de pază, Impărat și proletar, Rugăciunea unui Dac, Ânger și Demon).

Dacă totuș am publicat și aceste poesii impreună cu celelalte așa cum se găsesc, am făcut-o dintr'un simțimănt de datorie literară. Trebuiau să devie mai ușor accesibile pentru iubitorii de literatura noastră toate scrierile poetice, chiar și cele începătoare, a le unui autor, care a fost înzestrat cu darul de a întrupà într'o frumuseță de forme, subt al cărei farmec limba romănă pare a primi o nouă viață.

București, Decemvrie 1883

T. MAIORESCU

6

PREFACE TO THE FIRST EDITION

The present collection of Eminescu's poetry includes all those poems which have appeared in "Convorbiri Literare" over the last twelve years as well as others which have, until now, remained in manuscript from in private possession.

Publication is taking place in the poet's absence from the country. He has always been too unconcerned and unambitious about the future fate of his work to have been persuaded to work on a similar collection himself, despite the insistence of his literary friends.

The poems, as they appear in the following pages, have not been reviewed by Eminescu and do not, therefore, include the corrections he intended to make to them, in particular to the earlier ones (Venus and Madonna, Mortua Est, Egypt, Night, Guardian Angel, Emperor and Proletarian, A Dacian's Prayer, Angel and Demon).

Nevertheless, if I have published these latter poems along with the others as they stand, I have done so out of a sense of duty to literature. Lovers of our literature had to be offered easier access to all the poetic works, even the early ones, of a writer who has been endowed with the gift to substantiate beauty, under whose spell the Roumanian language appears to be reborn.

Bucharest, December 1883

T. MAIORESCU

Translated into English by Angela Clark, B. A. (Hons) First Class, University of London.

POETUL EMINESCU
(fragmente)

Tênĕra generație română se află astăzi sub influența operei poetice a lui Eminescu.

Se cuvine dar să ne dăm samă de individualitatea omului, care a personificat in sine cu atâta strălucire ultima fază a poesiei române de astăzi.

Viața lui externă e simplă de povestit, și nu credem, că în tot decursul ei să fi avut vre-o intîmplare din afară o înrîurire mai insemnată asupra lui. Ce a fost și ce a devenit Eminescu, este resultatul geniului sĕu innăscut, care erà prea puternic in a sa proprie ființă, încât să'l fi abătut vre-un contact cu lumea de la drumul sĕu firesc. Ar fi fost crescut Eminescu in România sau in Franța și nu in Austria și in Germania; ar fi moștenit sau ar fi agonisit el mai multă sau mai puțină avere; ar fi fost așezat în hierarchia Statului la o posiție mai înaltă; ar fi intîlnit in viața lui sentimentală orce alte figuri omenești: Eminescu remânea acelaș, soarta lui nu s'ar fi schimbat.

Născut la 20 Decembrie 1849* în satul Ipotești lîngă Botoșani, primind prima invețătură in gimnasiul din Cernĕuți, părăsind la 1864 școala pentru a se luà după trupa de teatru a d-nei Fanni Tardini prin România și prin Transilvania, părăsind și această trupă pentru a se aruncà cu cea mai mare incordare in studii felurite la Viena, susținut acolo și la Berlin in parte prin contribuțiile unor amici literari, numit între 1874 și 1876 revisor scolar și bibliotecar la Iași, [...] însărcinat apoi cu redacția ziarului « Timpul », incălzit din vreme, dar numai sporadic, de farmecul unor femei, de la care au remas in poesiile lui câte-va urme de pĕr bălai, de ochi întunecați, de mâne reci, de un știu ce și nu știu cum, (...) Eminescu moare la 15 Iunie 1889. [...]

Ceea ce caracterizează mai ântâi de toate personalitatea lui Eminescu, este o așa de coverșitoare inteligență, ajutată de o memorie, căreia nimic din cele ce-și intipărise vreodată nu'i mai scăpa, [...] încât lumea, în care trăia el după firea lui și fără nici o silă, erà aproape exclusiv lumea ideilor generale ce și le însușise și le avea pururea la îndemână. În aceeaș proporție

---

* 15 Ianuarie 1850

THE POET EMINESCU
(Fragments)

The younger generation in Roumania today is under the influence of the poetic works of Eminescu.

It is, therefore, an opportune time for us to consider the individuality of a man who has become such a brilliant personification of the most recent wave in contemporary Roumanian poetry.

The superficial details of his life are easy to relate; we do not believe that any one particular incident which took place in his lifetime made a more lasting impression on him than did any other. What Eminescu was, and what he became, was the result of his innate genius which had such profound control over him that no personal contact could have diverted him from his natural course in life. If Eminescu had received his higher education in Roumania or in France and not in Austria and Germany; if he had inherited or amassed more or less wealth; if he had been given a higher position in the state hierarchy; if he had been acquainted with different people in his private life: Eminescu would have still been the same, his destiny would have been no different.

He was born on 20th December 1849 * in the village of Ipotești near Botoșani. He received his elementary education at the German school in Cernăuți which he left in 1864 to follow the Fanny Tardini theatrical troupe throughout Roumania and Transylvania. He left the troupe behind to take up, with the greatest enthusiasm, diverse studies in Vienna and Berlin, financially supported in part by the contributions of some of his literary friends. Between 1874 and 1876, he was appointed school inspector and subsequently librarian in Iași ... later he was given an editing post at the newspaper « Timpul ». He was, from time to time, animated by the charms of several women, traces of whom can be found in his poems — flaxen hair, dark eyes, cold hands ... Eminescu died on the 15th June 1889.

The most characteristic trait of Eminescu's personality was an overwhelming intelligence, bolstered by a memory from which no fact which

---

* 15th January 1850

tot ce erà cas individual, întîmplare externă, convenție socială, avere sau neavere, rang sau nivelare obștească, și chiar soarta externă a persoanei sale ca persoană îi erau indiferente. A vorbi de miseria materială a lui Eminescu însemnează a întrebuința o expresie nepotrivită cu individualitatea lui și pe care el cel d'intâi ar fi respins-o. Cât i-a trebuit lui Eminescu pentru ca să trăiască în accepțiunea materială a cuvêntului, a avut el totdeauna. Grijile existenței nu l-au cuprins niciodată; cînd nu câștiga singur, îl susținea tatăl său și-l ajutau amicii. Ear recunoașterile publice le-a desprețuit totdeauna.

Vre un premiu academic pentru poesiile lui Eminescu, de a cărui lipsă se plânge o revistă germană din București? Dar Eminescu ar fi intîmpinat o asemenea propunere cu un ris homeric sau, după disposiția momentului, cu acel suris de indulgență miloasă ce'l avea pentru nimicurile lumești. — Regina României, admiratoare a poesiilor lui, a dorit să'l vadă, și Eminescu a avut mai multe convorbiri literare cu Carmen Sylva. L-am vêzut și eu la Curte și l-am vêzut pêstrând și aici simplitatea încântătoare ce o avea in toate raporturile sale omenești. Dar când a fost vorba să i se confere o distincție onorifică, un bene-merenti sau nu știu ce altă decorație, el s'a impotrivit cu energie. Rege el insuș al cugetării omenești, care alt Rege ar fi putut să '1 distingă? Și aceasta nu din vre-o vanitate a lui, de care erà cu desăvîrșire lipsit, nu din sumeția unei inteligențe excepționale, de care numai el singur nu erà știutor, ci din naivitatea unui geniu cuprins de lumea ideală, pentru care orce coborîre în lumea convențională erà o supărare și o nepotrivire firească.

Cine 'și dă samă de o asemenea figură, va ințelege indată, că nu'l puteai prinde pe Eminescu cu interesele care ademenesc pe cei mai mulți oameni. Luxul stării materiale, ambiția, iubirea de glorie nu au fost în nici un grad obiectul preocupărilor sale. Să fi avut ca redactor al « Timpului » mai mult decât a avut, să fi avut mai puțin: pentru micele lui trebuințe materiale tot atât erà. ...

Și nici munca specială a unui redactor de ziar nu credem că trebuie privită la Eminescu ca o sforțare impusă de nevoie unui spirit recalcitrant. Eminescu era omul cel mai silitor, vecinic cetind, meditând, scriind. Lipsit de orce interes egoist, el se interesà cu atât mai mult la toate manifestările vieții intelectuale, fie scrierile vre unui prieten, fie cetirea a tot ce se publică în literatura romană, fie studierea mișcării filosofice în Europa, fie izvoarele istorice, despre care avea cunoștința cea mai amênunțită, fie luptele politice din țară. A se ocupà cu vre una din aceste chestii, a cugetà și a scrie asupra lor, erà lucrul cel mai potrivit cu felul spiritului sêu. Și energia, cu care a redactat « Timpul », înălțimea de vederi, ce apare în toate articolele lui, puterea neuitată, cu care incontra frazei despre *naționalismul* liberal al partidului de la guvern a opus importanța elementului autohton, sunt o davadă pentru aceasta.

10

impressed him was ever forgotten. He lived comfortably in a world which was pleasing to him — almost exclusively a world of general ideas which he had assimilated and which were always at his disposal. Similarly, he was indifferent to any individual event or peripheral occurrence in his life, to social convention, wealth or the lack of it, class distinction and even to his own apparent fate. To speak of Eminescu's material poverty would mean to employ an expression alien to his own character and he would have been the first person to deny its relevance. Eminescu always had sufficient means from which to live, in the material sense of the word. He never worried about life's basic necessities; if he did not earn enough himself, his father or his friends helped him out. He never valued public recognition.

Should Eminescu have been conferred an academic award for his poetry, a fact which was unrealized and complained about by a German magazine published in Bucharest? Eminescu would, however, have greeted such a proposition with Homeric laughter, or according to his mood at the time, with the same compassionate and indulgent smile he had for all worldly trifles — the Queen of Romania, a great admirer of his poetry requested to see him and Eminescu had many literary discussions with Carmen Sylva. I had the occasion to see him at the Court and noticed that even there he preserved the delightful simplicity with which he conducted all areas of his life. However, when the question arose of conferring an honorary distinction on him he was vigorously opposed to the idea. Himself the king of human thought, which other king was capable of honouring him? This was not, however, because of personal vanity, a trait absent from his character, nor because of his exceptional intelligence, of which only he himself was not conscious, but was the result of the naivety of a genius encapsulated in an ideal world, for whom any descent into the material world was a burden and contrary to his nature.

Whoever can conceive of such a personality will immediately understand why Eminescu could not be captivated by the interests which prove attractive to the majority of people. A life of luxury, ambition, desire for fame, were not the reasons behind his preoccupations. If as an editor for « Timpul », he had earned more or less than he did, it would have made no difference to his few material needs.

As far as the editing work for a newspaper was concerned, we do not believe that it should be regarded as an effort imposed on a recalcitrant personality. Eminescu was a most diligent man, always reading, reflecting, writing. Devoid of any trace of egoism, he was therefore all the more interested in all expressions of intellectual life; the writings of a friend, reading everything published in Romanian literature, studying the European philosophical movements or historical documents — about which he had a most detailed knowledge — or the political struggles within the country. Taking up one of these matters, thinking about it and then writing down his thoughts

11

Cu o aşa natură, Eminescu găseà un element firesc pentru activitatea lui în toate situaţiile, în care a fost pus. La bibliotecă, pentru a'şi spori comoara deja imensă a memoriei sale; ca revisor scolar, pentru a stărui cu limpezimea spiritului său asupra nouelor metode de inveţământ; in cercul de amici literari, pentru a se bucurà fără invidie sau a rîde fără rěutate de scrierile cetite; la redacţia « Timpului », pentru a biciui fraseologia neaděvărată şi a formulà sintesa unei direcţii istorice naţionale: în toate aceste ocupări şi sfere Eminescu se aflà fără silă în elementul sěu. [. . .] Viaţa lui erà neregulată; adesea se hrănea numai cu narcotice şi excitante; abus de tutun şi de cafea, nopţi petrecute în cetire şi scriere, zile întregi petrecute fără mâncare, şi apoi de odată la vreme neobişnuită, după miezul nopţii, mâncare, şi băuturi fără alegere şi fără měsură: aşa era viaţa lui Eminescu [. . .]

Dacă ne-ar întreba cine-va: a fost fericit Eminescu? am răspunde: cine e fericit? Dar dacă ne-ar întrebà: a fost nefericit Eminescu? am răspunde cu toată convingerea: nu! Ce e drept, el erà pětruns de ideile lui Schopenhauer, erà prin urmare pesimist. Dar acest pesimism nu erà redus la plângerea mărginită a unui egoist nemulţumit cu soarta sa particulară, ci erà eterizat sub forma mai senină a melancoliei pentru soarta omenirii indeobşte; şi chiar acolo, unde din poesia lui străbate indignarea in contra epigonilor şi a demagogilor inselători, avem a face cu un simţiment estetic, ear nu cu o amărăciune personală. Eminescu, din punct de vedere al egoismului cel mai nepăsător om ce şi'l poate închipui cine-va, precum nu putea fi atins de un simţiment prea intensiv al fericirii, nu putea fi nici expus la o prea mare nefericire. Seninătatea abstractă — eacă nota lui caracteristică, in melancolie ca şi in veselie. [. . .]

Când venea in mijlocul nostru cu naivitatea sa ca de copil, care êi câştigase de mult inima tuturor, şi ne aducea ultima poesie ce o făcuse, o refăcuse, o refinase, căutând mereu o formă mai perfectă, o cetea par'că ar fi fost o lucrare străină de el. Nici odată nu s'ar fi gîndit măcar să o publice; publicarea êi erà indiferentă, unul sau altul din noi trebuie să'i ia manuscrisul din mână şi să'l dea la « Convorbiri ».

Şi dacă pentru poesiile lui, în care şi-a întrupat sub o formă aşa de minunată quintesenţa cugetărilor şi simţirilor, se mulţumeà cu emoţiunea estetică a unui mic cerc de amici, fără a se gîndi la nici o satisfacţie de amor-propriu; dacă el se considerà oarecum ca organul accidental, prin care insăş poesia se manifestă, aşa încât ar fi primit cu aceeaş mulţumire să se fi manifestat prin altul: ne este permis a conchide, nu numai că erà nepăsător pentru intîmplările vieţei externe, dar şi chiar că în relaţiile lui pasionale erà de un caracter cu totul nebicinuit. Cuvintele de amor fericit sau nefericit nu se pot aplica lui Eminescu in accepţiunea de toate zilele. Nicio individualitate femeiască nu'l putea captivà şi ţinea cu desăvîrşire in mărginirea ei. Ca şi Leopardi în Aspasia, el nu vedea în femeia iubită decât copia imperfectă a unui prototip nerealizabil. Il iubea intêmplătoarea copie sau il părăsea,

12

was perfectly suited to his nature. The energy with which he edited "Timpul", the loftiness of his insight, which is evident in all his articles, the unforgettable power with which he set down the importance of the national element as opposed to the relative principles of the liberal nationalists upheld by the government party, these bear witness to this.

Eminescu's character was such that he felt at home in any work situation in which he found himself. At the liberary, he increased the immense wealth of his memory; as school inspector, he insisted, with clarity of vision, on the implementation of more modern teaching methods; in his circle of literary friends, he selflessly delighted in, or kindly laughed about, the pieces read out by the others; as editor at "Timpul", he severely criticised the false phraseology of the time and synthesised a national trend in our history; in all these endeavours and areas of life, Eminescu found himself, quite comfortably, in his element.

His life was somewhat unstable: he often lived only on narcotics and stimulants; excesses of tobacco and coffee, whole nights spent reading and writing, days at a time without food, then, all of a sudden, at some odd hour after midnight, he would eat and drink indiscriminately and excessively: such was Eminescu's life.

If somebody was to ask the question: was Eminescu happy? We would say: is anyone happy? But if someone asked: was Eminescu unhappy? We would answer, quite firmly: No! It is true, however, that he was deeply influenced by the ideas of Schopenhauer, and was, therefore, a pessimist. But this pessimism was not merely the narrow-minded complaint of an egoist, unsatisfied with his particular fate, but was rather translated into a peaceful feeling of melancholy as regards the fate of humanity itself; even in those poems in which he expresses his indignation against the epignoes or the untrustworthy demagogues, this is not personal bitterness but rather an aesthetic sentiment. Eminescu, from an egoistical point of view, was the most detached person one could imagine, and just as he was oblivious to intense feelings of happiness, he could not be affected by extreme unhappiness. Serene idealism — that was his characteristic trait, in both sadness and happiness.

When he attended our meetings (with his childlike naivety which won him many people's hearts, and brought us the latest poem he had written, rewritten and refined — always striving for the most perfect from — he would read it to us as if it were alien to him. He would never even have thought about publishing it: its publication was irrelevant: one of us would have to take the manuscript out of his hand and submit it to "Convorbiri".

As regards his poetry, in which his quintessential thoughts and feelings were wonderfully embodied, he was content that a small circle of friends were touched by them, without a thought for his own self-esteem; if he considered himself as an accidental medium through which poetry itself

tot copie rěmâneà, şi el se refugià cu melancolie impersonală într'o lume mai potrivită cu el, in lumea cugetării şi a poesiei. De aici « Luceaferul » cu versurile de la sfârşit.

> Ce'ţi pasă ţie, chip de lut,
>   Dac'oi fi eu sau altul?
> Trăind in cercul vostru strimt,
>   Norocul vě petrece;
> Ci eu in lumea mea mă simt
>   Nemuritor şi rece.

Bucureşti, Octombrie 1889

T. MAIORESCU

14

found expression, he would have been just as happy if it had been expressed by somebody else: we feel we can justifiably conclude that not only was he indifferent to life's outward events but he was also unusually so in love affairs. Happiness or unhappiness in love are words which cannot be applied to Eminescu in their everyday meaning... No one single woman ever managed to win and keep him completely to herself. Like Leopardi in Aspasia, the woman he loved was only an imperfect copy of an unattainable prototype. Whether the copy of the moment loved him or left him, she remained merely a copy, while he ensconced himself melancolically into a world which was closer to his own spirit, that of reflection and poetry. Hence Lucifer and the closing lines,

> "O what care you, fair face of clay,
>   If it be he or I?
> Still earth shall only earth remain
>   Let luck its course unfold
> And I in my own kingdom reign
>   Immutable and cold".

T. MAIORESCU

Bucharest, October 1889

Translated into English by **Angela Clark, B. B.** (Hons) First Class, University of London.

CUVÎNT ÎNAINTE

În această versiune în limba engleză a poeziilor lui Eminescu, am folosit în materie de text ediția Maiorescu și am urmat în privința ordinii și aranjamentului poeziilor ediția II, cu excepția poeziei „Departe sînt de tine". După opinia mea, locul acesteia este imediat după poezia „Singurătate" și nu în altă parte, cum a făcut Maiorescu. Astfel sîntem foarte aproape de Eminescu, care la 1 martie 1878 în „Convorbiri Literare" considera versurile începînd cu „Departe sînt de tine . . ." ca o continuare a poeziei „Singurătate" și le-a inclus în ea. După poezia „Criticilor mei", cu care se încheie ediția II Maiorescu, am adăugat unele poezii din alte ediții Maiorescu, precum și cîteva poezii din perioada de adolescență a lui Eminescu care nu apar la Maiorescu.

Am ales ediția II, deoarece cifra „doi" reprezintă ziua și luna de naștere (2 februarie) a iubitei mele „mămicuțe", căreia doresc să-i dedic această activitate literară.

Cuvintele doina, toaca, cobza și candela sînt date așa cum apar în original. Am considerat că un substituent englez le-ar fi lipsit de întreaga lor semnificație și culoare.

În ceea ce privește folosirea lui Lucifer în loc de Luceafărul, s-ar putea obiecta că Lucifer denumește diavolul, nu așa precum a face Luceafărul, o personificare a prințului luminii, simbolizat de o stea. Nu este corect. În mitologia engleză, Lucifer ține un rol aproape identic cu cel ocupat de Luceafăr în cea română, anume acela al prințului luminii, simbolizat de către o stea. A traduce Luceafărul prin simpla denumire de evening-star ar însemna a-l lipsi de orice fel de personalitate.

Cîteva cuvinte sînt necesare în ceea ce privește accentul. Peste tot în lucrările sale, se constată că Eminescu preferă simplitatea, claritatea și încrederea în propriul simț înnăscut al exprimării poetice, decît o aderare rigidă la vreo formă metrică restrictivă oarecare. Peste tot în lucrările sale, ești impresionat de extrema flexibilitate în materie de metru. Găsești mereu, de exemplu, rime pe penultima urmînd direct după rime pe ultima și vice versa. În mîinile unui poet de talia lui Eminescu, o asemenea libertate a dat rezultate minunate, și acest motiv contribuie în mare măsură a da poeziilor o remarcabilă fluiditate și o grație ușoară ce atît

---

Traducerea în română—Ion Kleante Gheorghiu.

16

FOREWORD

In this English version of Eminescu's poems, I have followed the text of the Maiorescu edition and as far as order and arrangement are concerned I have used the second edition, except for the poem *Now Far I Am From You*. In my opinion this poem should be placed immediately after *Solitude*, not as it was placed by Maiorescu. In this way we are very close to Eminescu who considered, when publishing *Solitude* in *Convorbiri Literare* of March 1, 1878, that the lines commencing *Now far I am from you ...* are a continuation of the above poem and therefore attached to it. After the poem *To the Critics*, which closes Maiorescu's second edition, I have added some poems from other Maiorescu editions and some dating from the period of Eminescu's adolescence which do not appear in Maiorescu.

I have chosen the second edition seeing that *two* represents my beloved *mămicuța's* birthday; she was born on the second day of the second month (February 2) and it is to her that I want to dedicate my literary activity.

The words *doina*[1], *toaca*[2], *cobza*[3] and *candela*[4] are given as they appear in the original. I have considered that English substitutes would rob them of all significance and colour.

With regard to the use of *Lucifer* in place of *Luceafărul*, it could be objected that Lucifer denotes the devil and not, like *Luceafărul*, a personification of the prince of light, symbolized by a star. This is incorrect. In English mythology, *Lucifer* holds a place almost identical to that which *Luceafărul* holds in the Roumanian one; namely that of the prince of light, visibly symbolized by a star. To translate *Luceafărul* by the simple designation of *evening-star* would be to deprive it of all personality.

A few words may not be out of place here with regard to accent. Everywhere throughout his works, Eminescu is found to prefer simplicity, clarity and reliance upon his genuinely divine inborn sense of poetic expression to rigid adherence to any limiting metrical form. Everywhere in his poems one is struck by his extreme flexibility in metre. One continually finds, for instance, rhymes upon the penultimate following directly upon rhymes upon the ultimate and vice-versa. Unhampered freedom of this sort in the hands of a poet of such stature as Eminescu has given truly wonderful results, and it is very largely for this reason that his poems possess that remarkable fluidity and easy grace which so often give them the power and simplicity of a spoken word. It is this charac-

17

de deseori le conferă puterea și simplitatea unui cuvînt vorbit. Această caracteristică permite poeziilor sale să fie interpretate cu veracitate, nu numai de înțeles și formă, ci și de culoare și atmosferă, ceea ce nu se poate spune decît despre operele puținilor poeți.

În limba engleză, aproape toate cuvintele care exprimă formele primare ale naturii, și care se află la temeliile poeticei eminesciene, fiind de origine foarte veche, în cea mai mare parte din rădăcini anglo-saxone, celtice și germanice vechi, sînt monosilabe. Pe de altă parte în limba română inversul apare aproape invariabil. Pentru mai multă claritate, dau cîteva exemple. Dintre cuvintele relative la natură, ce apar cel mai frecvent în poeziile lui Eminescu pe primul loc se află următoarele, copac, ramură, crenguță, frunză, pasăre, pîrîu, piatră, stîncă, faleză, pămînt, soare, lună, stea, țărînă, mare, cer, zi, noapte, lumină, întuneric etc. Acestea (lista ar putea, desigur, să fie continuată la infinit) sînt toate monosilabe în engleză, în timp ce echivalentul lor românesc este polisilabic. Cu excepția cuvîntului body, numele părților corpului omenesc dovedesc sceeași divergență foot, leg, knee, calf, thigh, waist, arm, hand, skin, face, eye, ear, mouth, lip, cheek, chin etc. De asemenea emoțiile și altele love, hate, faith, hope, fear, grief, joy, pain etc., etc., etc . . . Dacă Eminescu ar fi aderat în mod pedant la vreo formă poetică rigidă, toate cuvinte primare ale limbii noastre, evident, ar fi fost eliminate din interpretarea englezească și rezultatul ar fi fost tocmai totala pierdere a acelei simplități naturale care este atît de remarcabilă la Eminescu.

Această diferență flagrantă de lungime a cuvintelor în cele două limbi a provocat un număr mai mare de cuvinte pentru un număr identic de silabe în engleză, față de original; o diferență ce nu pare să aibă vreo importanța în ceea ce privește rezultatul final. Evitînd mereu aceste cuvinte fundamentale și preferînd pe acele de origină mai tîrzie în limba engleză, apprehension în loc de fear, aspiration în loc de hope ș.a.m.d., s-ar fi putut evita cu ușurință acest inconvenient, într-o oarecare măsură, dar rezultatul ar fi fost o pierdere de asemănare cu originalul, și de asemenea a unei părți din valoarea poetică. Mai degrabă s-ar spune că această diferență în raportul lungimii cuvintelor a fost binevenită, căci a permis în engleză mobilitate și amplitudine fără de care ar fi fost imposibilă să se păstreze, într-o oarecare măsură, parfumul special și frumusețea naturală a acestui mare poet român .. a acestui mare poet universal.

Am reușit să realizez această versiune în limba engleză a acestor poezii ale lui Eminescu datorită profesorului meu Ion Kleante Gheorghiu, care m-a ajutat să-mi îmbunătățesc stăpînirea limbii, făcîndu-mă să gust frumusețea și subtilitățile sale. El mi-a permis cu amabilitate să consult bogatul său set de dicționare.

Interesul meu pentru literatură a fost stîrnit în cursul primilor mei ani de șocală de către profesoara Natalia Mirescu, a fost întreținut de profesorii mei de română ce au urmat și desăvîrșit de actuala profesoară Maria Pavnotescu de la liceul Nicolae Bălcescu.

teristic which allows his poems to be interpreted with veracity, not only of meaning and form, but also of colour and atmosphere, which the work of few poets will allow.

Almost all the words which apply to the primary forms of nature, and which are at the foundation of Eminescu's poetry, being of ancient origin in English — for the most part of Anglo-Saxon, Celtic and Old Germanic stock — they are monosyllables. In Roumanian, on the other hand, the reverse is almost as invariable. A few examples will make this clear. Among the words which are found more often in Eminescu's poems, the following regarding nature certainly come first: *tree, branch, twig, leaf, bird, spring, brook, stone, rock, cliff, ground, soil, sun, moon, star, earth, sea, sky, day, night, light, dark* etc. These (and the list could, of course, be continued almost indefinitely) are all mono-syllables in English, while their equivalents in Roumanian, without exception, are polysylla-bles. With the exception of *body* itself, the names of the parts of the human body show the same divergence: *foot, leg, knee, calf, thigh, waist, arm, hand, skin, face, eye, ear, mouth, lip, cheek, chin,* etc. Of the emotions and so on: *love, hate, faith, hope, fear, grief, joy, pain,* etc., etc., etc ... Had Eminescu therefore pedantically adhered to some rigid poetic form, for instance a rhyme upon the penultimate, all these primary words of our language would, quite obviously, have been eliminated from the English interpretation, and the result would have been an entire loss of precisely that natural simplicity for which Eminescu is most remarkable.

This marked difference in word length between the two languages has resulted in a greater number of words for the same number of syllables in English than in the original: a difference which seems to be of little, if any detriment to the work in hand. By consistenly avoiding these fundamental words and preferring those of later origin in the English language, *apprehension to fear, aspiration to hope,* and so on, this difference in the precise number of words to the line could easily have been overcome to some extent, but the result would have been a loss of all resemblance to the original, and of every atom of poetic value as well. Rather has the above difference in the relative word length in the two languages been welcome, for it has allowed the English language a mobility and amplitude without which it would have been impossible to retain to any appreciable extent the peculiar fragrance and natural beauty of this great Roumanian poet, of this great universal poet.

I could achieve this English version of Eminescu's poems thanks to my coach, Ion Kleante Gheorghiu, who helped me to enhance my command of the language, making me enjoy its beauty and subtleties. He kindly allowed me to consult his rich set of dictionaries.

My concern with literature was aroused during my early school-years by my teacher Natalia Mirescu, kept alive by my following teachers of Roumanian and enhanced by my present teacher Maria Pavnotescu of Lycée Nicolae Bălcescu.

My literary preoccupations have not interfered with my study of exact sciences the background of my future profession. I was skilfully initiated in this field by Vera Sofronie, my teacher of mathematics at the Silvestru school. At present my teachers,

Am urmărit tot timpul ca preocupările mele literare să nu-mi afecteze studiul științelor exacte, baza viitoarei mele profesiuni. Am fost inițiat cu grijă în acest domeniu de profesoara de matematică de la școala generală Silvestru, Vera Sofronie. Actualmente, profesorii Gheorghe Caloianu (matematică) și Traian Geangu (fizică) se pricep în a-mi întreține interesul pentru aceste științe.

Dar sînt conștient că datorez totul iubiților mei părinți — și mai ales mamei mele — care-și consacră toate forțele spre a mă pregăti pentru o viață activă și utilă în societate.

Gheorghe Caloianu (mathematics) and Traian Geangu (physics) know how to keep alive my interest in these sciences.

But I am aware that I owe everything to my beloved parents — and particularly to my mother — who devote all their forces to preparing me for an active and useful life in society.

Cornelia M. Popescu

---

1 *Doina*   = *melancholy Roumanian folk song.*
2 *Toaca*   = *bell board or simandron — suspended narrow board rhythmically, rapidly hit with small hammer(s) by monks or nuns to call the congregation to the office.*
3 *Cobza*   = *ancient string instrument used as accompaniment instrument when singing romances and love songs.*
4 *Candela* = *votive light; perpetually buring dim light in remembrance of beloved persons.*

SOLITUDE

With the curtains drawn together,
At my table of rough wood,
And the firelight flickering softly,
Do I fall to thoughtful mood.

5 Flocks and flocks of sweet illusions,
Memories the mind recalls,
And they softly creep like crickets
Through time's grey and crumbled walls;

Or they drop with gentle patter
10 On the pavement of the soul,
As does wax before God's altar
From the sacred candles roll.

About the room in every corner
Silver webs the spiders sew,
15 While among the dusty bookshelves
Furtive mice soft come and go.

And I gaze towards the ceiling
That so many times I saw,
And I listen how the bindings
20 With their tiny teeth they gnaw.

O, how often have I wanted
My worn lyre aside to lay;
From poetry and solitude
At last my thoughts to turn away.

25 But again the mice, the crickets,
With their small and rustling tread,
Awake in me familiar longings
And with poetry fill my head.

Once in a while, alas too rarely,
30 When my lamp is burning late,
Suddenly my heart beats wildly
For I hear the latch-bar grate.

It is *She*. My dusky chamber
In a moment seems to glow;
35 As if an icon's holy lustre
Did o'er life's threshold flow.

And I know not how the moments
Have the heart away to sneak,
While we whisper low our loving,
40 Hand in hand, and cheek to cheek.

NOW FAR I AM FROM YOU

Now far I am from you, before my fire alone,
And read again the hours that so silently have gone,
And it seems that eighty years beneath my feet did glide,
That I am old as winter, that maybe you have died.
5 The shadows of the past swift stream across life's floor
The tale of all times, nothings that now exist no more;
While the wind with clumsy fingers softly fumbles at the blind
And sadly spins the fibre of the story in my mind . . .
I see you stand before me in a mist that does enfold,
10 Your eyes are full of tears and your fingers long and cold;
About my neck caressing your arms you gently ply
And it seems you want to speak to me, yet only sigh.
And thus I clasp entranced my all, my world of grace,
And both our lives are joined in that supreme embrace . . .
15 Oh, let the voice of memory remain for ever dumb,
Forget the joy that was, but that nevermore will come,
Forget how after an instant you thrust my arms aside,
For now I'm old and lonely, and maybe you have died.

COME DEAR, SET YOUR WORLD APART

Come dear, set your world apart,
And on me yourself bestow;
Even should I take your heart,
No one in the world would know.

5 Come, let us awandering leave
Down steep winding sylvan ways
And amidst the twilight eve
Listen what the forest says.

O'er our path amidst the trees
10 Stars will silently appear;
Come dear one, except for these,
No one in the world will hear.

Your gold hair you will untwist
And most lovely you will be;
15 Should I hug you, don't resist,
No one in the world will see.

Now the distant bagpipes' croon
Does the sacred night invade,
While appears the climbing moon
20 O'er the silver beech-tree's glade.

And amidst the boughs her light
Does enchanted shadows trace;
And I lose my senses quite
Gazing dear upon your face.

25 But you sigh and turn away,
You would dwell, yet do not dare,
You would go, and yet you stay,
Angel you with hanging hair.

Look, the water's iridescent
30 Where the moon in splendour shines.
And within the lake her crescent
Its sweet loneliness enshrines.

On its surface starlight trembles,
Ripples through the rushes creep;
35 In its dreams the world assembles
And it cannot fall asleep.

While your lovely face beguiling
Holds it like a mirror there,
What do you regard in smiling?
40 Don't you know that you are fair?

Blue the starlit heavens high,
Stars that in the water glow,
On the lake and in the sky,
Stars above and stars below.

45 Here the lime-tree's scent is blown,
Here the twilight casts its spell,
And we two are quite alone,
And so happy words can't tell.

Lonely hangs the moon at rest
50   O'er the stream where vapour furls,
And I close you to my breast
Maiden mine, with golden curls.

AND IF...

And if the branches tap my pane
And the poplars whisper nightly.
It is to make me dream again
I hold you to me tightly.

5 And if the stars shine on the pond
And light its sombre shoal,
It is to quench my mind's despond
And flood with peace my soul.

And if the clouds their tresses part
10 And does the moon outblaze,
It is but to remind my heart
I long for you always.

CUPID ...

Cupid, dreadfully spoiled rascal,
Many a hoax stored in his head,
With the children romps and scampers,
With the ladies sleeps in bed.

5 From the daylight like a brigand
He will take great pains to hide;
But at dark he'll try your window
And if it's open slip inside.

Bits of string and bows and arrows
10 That's of what his wealth is made.
Generous when no one needs him,
Stingy should you ask his aid.

Late at night he'll rob your bookcase,
Read some volume doctrinaire,
15 And maybe between the pages
Find a thread of golden hair.

With strange thoughts, they cannot master,
Does he lead young minds astray;
Then before a lighted icon
20 All night long he'll kneel and pray.

Oft some little girl in whispers
Does in him her soul confide,
And all night they sleep together
Like two pigeons side by side.

25 Petulant he is and heartless,
Winsome too, and full of guile,
And his eyes will sometimes sparkle
Roguish as a widow's smile.

Graceful throat and rounded shoulder,
30 Here where maiden breast expands,
He will take a double armful
And will hide it with his hands.

While if you should beg him nicely,
Quite enough a scamp is he
35 Just to part the veil a little
And a moment let you see.

WHY DO YOU WAIL, O FOREST TREES

(In the folk style)

« Why do you wail, o forest trees,
Forest, without rain or breeze,
Your branches ill at ease? »

« How indeed should I not wail
5 When the hours of summer fail !
Nights grow longer, days get short,
On my branches few leaves caught,
And the winds with bitter sword
Drive my choristers abroad;
10 Autumn winds that forests flay,
Winter near, spring far away.
How indeed should I not groan
When my singing birds have flown,
And across the frozen sky
15 Flocks of swallows hurry by,
And with them my fancies fly
Leaving me alone to sigh;
Hurry on as time in flight
Turning day half into night,
20 Time that o'er the forest rings
With a fluttering of wings ...
And they pass and leave me cold,
Nude and shivering and old;
For my thoughts with them have flown,
25 And with them my gladness gone ! »

MELANCHOLY

It seemed that midst the clouds a gate was opened wide
Through which the pallid empress of waning night did ride.
O sleep, o sleep in silence, where thousand torches loom,
Wrapped in your silver garments, high in your crystal tomb,
5 Your sepulcher of heaven, of sky's arc opaline,
O you beloved, and worshipped, fair moon of night the queen!
Unbounded is the kigdom that dreams beneath your haze,
What villages and valleys are lighted by your rays;
The sky is all asparkle, and 'neath your pallid gleam
10 The lonely ruined castle has walls of chalk it seem.
The empty graveyard crouches beside the time-old church,
Its crosses leaning all ways, on one an owl aperch.
The belfry creaks, the *toaca* against it upright swings
As though some flying demon with dark transparent wings
15 Had touched it unexpectedly while lighting on the ground,
That it begins to tremble, and gives a wailing sound.

                        The church, a ruin lorn,
Is bowed and sad and empty, a place of shadows mourn;
And through it's gaping windows a moaning breeze is heard,
20 As though grey witches whispered and one could hear their word.
On pillars and on altar, and painted walls remain
Naught but the gloomy contours on which time spreads its stain.
For priest a criket chirps a sermon fine, obscure;
For sexton digs a woodworm eternal sepulture.

....

25   Faith sets up in its churches fair icons to the saints,
And in my soul sweet fancy a fairy legend paints;
But of time tossing billows, and wild tumultuous strain,
Naught but the gloomy contours and shadows now remain.
In vain I seek what happened in my exhausted mind.
30   A hoarsely prating cricket is all that I can find.
In vain my hand despairing upon my heart I clench,
Its stir is but a woodworm within the coffin bench.
When I look back on living, the past seems to unfold
As though it were a story by foreign lips retold.
35   As though I had not lived it, nor made of life a part.

Who is it then so softly this tale recites by heart
That I should pause to listen ... And laugh at what is said
As though it never happened? ... Maybe since long I'm dead!

A DACIAN'S PRAYER

When death did not exist, nor yet eternity,
Before the seed of life had first set living free,
When yesterday was nothing, and *time had not begun,*
And *one* included all things, and *all* was less than one,
5 When sun and moon and sky, the stars, the spinning earth
Were still part of the things that had not come to birth,
And You quite lonely stood... I ask myself with awe,
Who is this mighty God we bow ourselves before.

Ere yet the Gods existed already He was God
10 And out of endless water with fire the lightning shed;
He gave the Gods their reason, and joy to earth did bring,
He brought to man forgiveness, and set salvation's spring.
Lift up your hearts in worship, a song of praise enfreeing.
He is the death of dying, the primal birth of being.

15 To him I owe my eyes that I can see the dawn,
To him I owe my heart wherein is pity born;
Whene'er I hear the tempest, I hear him pass along
Midst multitude of voices raised in a holy song;
And yet of his great mercy I beg still one behest:
20 That I at last be taken to his eternal rest.

Be curses on the fellow who would my praise acclaim.
But blessings upon him who does my soul defame;

Believe no matter whom who slanders my renown,
Give power to the arm that lifts to strike me down;
25 Let him upon the earth above all others loom
Who steals away the stone that lies upon my tomb.

Hunted by humanity, let me my whole life fly
Until I feel from weeping my very eyes are dry;
Let everyone detest me no matter where I go,
30 Until from persecution myself I do not know;
Let misery and horror my heart transform to stone,
That I may hate my mother, in whose love I have grown;
Till hating and deciving for me with love will vie,
And I forget my suffering, and learn at last to die.

35 Dishonoured let me perish, an outcast among men;
My body less than worthy to block the gutter then,
And may, o God of mercy, a crown of diamonds wear
The one who gives my heart the hungry dogs to tear,
While for the one who in my face does callous fling a clod
40 In your eternal kingdom reserve a place, o God.

Thus only, gracious Father, can I requitance give
That you from your great bounty vouched me the joy to live
To gain eternal blessings my head I do not bow,
But rather ask that you in hating compassion show.
45 Till comes at last the evening, your breath will mine efface,
And into endless nothing I go, and leave no trace.

BEATS THE MOON UPON MY WINDOW

Beats the moon upon my window
Down the same untroubled lane.
Only you are never passing,
Nevermore beyond my pane.

5 And the same prune trees in blossom
Reach their branches o'er the fence,
But the hours the past has taken
Never shall again come thence.

Other is your soul's intention,
10 Other eyes you have today,
Only I who am unchanging
Tread for ever that same way.

O, how slim and young and graceful,
Secretly with paces slow,
15 Would you come to me at evening
'Neath the hidden hawthorn's bough.

While my arms were clasped about you
It seemed we from the earth had sped;
And we talked great things together,
20 Though not a word had either said.

Kisses were our single answer,
Many queries, just one task,
While about the world beyond us
Neither had the time to ask.

25 Aye, little I knew in youth's enchantment
That it is alike absurd
Or to lean against a shadow,
Or believe a woman's word.

And the air still moves my curtain
30 As it used in times of yore . . .
Moonlight down the lane uncertain,
Only you come nevermore.

HOW MANY A TIME, BELOVED...

How many a time, beloved, no longer do I know,
There seems to spread before me a sea of ice and snow;
And not a single star does in the heaven shine,
Only the yellow moon quite far away ... a sign.
5 While o'er the drifted waste of frozen ocean there
A bird with weary wings hangs in the winter air.
Its mate has gone ahead, and left it all alone,
Together with a flock that to the west has flown.
And so it gazes after, with tired, straining eyes,
10 But is no longer sorry now, nor glad ... and dies,
While do its parting dreams the happy past pursue.

. . . .

Day by day I'm farther, beloved one, from you,
And slowly, cold and darkness do take me for their prey ...
While you fly on for ever, midst time's eternal day.

O REMAIN, DEAR ONE...

« O remain, dear one, I love you,
Stay with me in my fair land,
For your dreamings and your longings
Only I can understand.

5 You, who like a prince reclining
O'er the pool with heaven starred;
You who gaze up from the water
With such earnest deep regard.

Stay, for where the lapping wavelets
10 Shake the tall and tasseled grass,
I will make you hear in secret
How the furtive chamois pass.

Oh, I see you wrapped in magic,
Hear your murmur low and sweet,
15 As you break the shallow water
With your slender naked feet;

See you thus amidst the ripples
Which the moon's pale beams engage,
And your years seem but an instant,
20 And each instant seems an age. »

Thus spake the woods in soft entreaty;
Arching boughs above me bent,
But I whistled high, and laughing
Out into the open went.

25 Now though e'en I roamed that country
How could I its charm recall...
Where has boyhood gone, I wonder,
With its pool and woods and all?

SEPARATION

To not forget our loving, should I a sign implore?
I'd ask for you, but dearest, you are your own no more.
Nor do I beg a flower from in your golden hair;
Forgetfulness, beloved, is but my single prayer.

5   Oh, what a sad sensation, when joy that soon did wane,
Not swift with it to vanish, but ever here remain!
Down quite a different valley does that same river fret;
The long and silent sameness of immutable regret
When through this life to wander it has been writ, it seem,
10 A dream made out of shadow, a shadow made of dream.
From now in my existence what interest can you hold?
Why should one count the ages that o'er the dead are rolled?
No matter when I die, this or some later day,
My wish is out o'the mind of all to I pass away,
15 And you forget the dream that our two hearts endears.
When you look back, beloved, upon the faded years,
Let in the depths of shadow my memory be gone,
As though we midst our loving each other had not known,
As though those hours of wonder in fact we did not live.
20 That I so deeply love you dear one can you forgive?
My face turned to the desert you left me all alone
And cold beneath my eyelids my eyes have turned to stone.
And when at last death's soil my body does reclaim,
Then who on earth will know me or know from whence I came?

25 A chant of lamentation within cold walls will chime
To beg for me in weeping the peace of endless time;
And I would fain that someone quite near to me then came
To whisper to me softly, beloved one, your name.
While then ... should they my body into the gutter throw,
30 Still that would be far better than what I suffer now.
Afar off in the distance a flock of crows arise
And darken all the heavens before my sightless eyes;
Beyond the earth's steep margin a hurricane does start,
Flinging to the world my dust and to the wind my heart.

35 Yet as in spring the blossom do you remain the while,
With gentle eyes and humid, and tender childish smile;
So much a child, yet seeming each day to younger grow,
And of my fate know nothing, as I too nothing know.

LEGENDARY QUEEN

Sparkling haze, across the heavens
Rising slow the silver moon,
She has gathered from the water
And upon the pastures strewn.

5   In the valley many flowers
On the cobwebs jewels strung,
Countless gems, of countless colours,
On the cloak of evening hung.

O'er the lake the clouds in passing
10 Cast a soft transparent shade,
Which the ripples rolling boulders
With their radiance invade.

Came at night a little maiden
Silently the reeds among,
15 And a rose of flaming scarlet
On the water surface flung.

For her own sweet image gazing,
Marvelled how the ripples stirred . . .
Ay, that lake is long enchanted
20 By the saint Mercury's word.

Flung a rose of flaming scarlet
That the water's mirror blurred . . .
Scarlet roses are enchanted
By the saint Venery's word.

25 Long she gazes. Hair soft golden,
O'er her face the moon's pale light,
While within her eyes of violet
All times fairy tales unite.

ODE

(in antique metre)

I little thought that I would learn to die;
Forever young, enveloped in my cloak,
My dreaming eyes I lifted to the star
                Of solitude.

5 When of a sudden you stood in my way,
On, anguish you, of nameless suffering sweet...
And to the dregs I dank the draught of death
                Unpardoning.

Miserably I burn alive like Nessus,
10 Or Hercules wrapped in his poisoned cloak;
The fire in me the boundless sea itself
                Could never quench.

By my own dreams consumed, I endless wail;
At my own pile I am consumed in flame,
15 Shall I then luminous one day return
                As does the Phœnix?

Tormenting eyes but vanish from my way,
Come to my breast again sad unconcern;
That I may die in peace at last, myself
                Give back to me.

MIDST THE DENSE OLD FOREST STOUT

(In the folk style)

Midst the dense old forest stout
All the merry birds fly out,
Quit the hazel thicket there
Out into the sunny air,
5 Round the pool grown high with sedge
Fly about the water's edge
Where, by little waves deflected,
On its shining face reflected,
Image of the moon is lying,
10 And of birds of passage flying,
And of stars and heavens blue,
And of swallows not a few,
And my darling's image too.

VENUS AND MADONNA

An ideal hidden in the night of an age that now no longer is,
An age when men in legend thought, and soke their thoughts in poet's
wise,
Oh, but I see you, hear you, know you, sweet and youthful promises
Born of a world with other stars, with other gods and other skies.

5   Venus, warmly gleaming marble, with eyes of stone that brightly shine,
With arms as smooth and gentle as the dream of some high poet king,
A goddess and a woman fair that in one body do combine,
A woman of whose beauty still e'en to the present day we sing.

Rafael, astray in dreams, as though in night's star-sparkling air,
10   His spirit drunken with their rays and spring's eternal wonder seen,
Espied your face, and dreaming heaven with fragrant moonlit gardens
fair
Did set you in the stars to reign, of all God's angels you the queen.

Upon an empty canvas he the sweet Madonna then did paint
With gleaming diadem of stars, a virgin smile lit in her eyes,
15   A pallid ray upon her cheek; a woman yet an angel saint
For in our visions do we see angels all in woman's guise.

And thus I, who in the night of a life of poetry lonely dwell,
Espied you, o barren woman, without soul and without fire
And of you have made an angel, sweet as secret magic spell,
20   When across a desert world luck and longing do conspire.

48

I saw your face corruption show, by lust's hot hunger drawn and pale,
I saw your lips depraved and bruised by passion's blinding violence,
And over your white shoulders bare I threw the poet's misty veil
And on your pallid cheeks I set a girlish glow of innocence.

25 I gave to you the radiance that lights with sparkling fairy
The sacred mien of praying nun, of pious child celestial;
Out of a demon made a saint, out of discord harmony,
And lit within your heart impure a virgin brilliance matinal.

Disillusion all is gone, the veil of dream is sadly torn,
30 Your frosty bloodless lips have touched to wakefulness my sleeping brow
And I have learned to gaze on you with endless pity and with scorn
My love for you, o demon child, grown cold and quite extinguished now.

I see you now a bacchant who a plaited myrtly wreath does wear
That you did from the pious head of some good martyr sinfully steal;
35 A martyr whose sweet virgin soul was saintly as fervent prayer,
While your delirious heart instead through endless bacchanal does reel.

As Rafael on canvas bare did the Madonna's portrait paint
With gleaming diadem of stars and eyes lit with a virgin smile,
So I a pallid mortal girl transformed into a deathless saint,
40 A girl with barren empty soul and body soiled, depraved and vile.

. . . .

You weep dear child? But don't you know that in your will the
                                        power lies
With but a single pleading glance my yearning heart again to bind?
I kneel down humbly at your feet and seek for pardon in your eyes,
I kiss your hands again, again and beg that I forgiveness find.

45 No, dry your eyes, dear one, don't weep, my accusations do not heed
For they were naught but empty lies, unfounded, wicked and unfair.
Why, were you demon, so much love would make you holy then indeed,
And I adore this demon saint with big blue eyes and golden hair.

SONNET

Loving in secret, I did silence hold
Deeming in this your clemency would dwell,
For when my searching eyes on yours fell
A world of shattered dreams they did behold.

5   I can no more. My aching love must tell
The mystery that does my heart enfold;
I wish I could drown within the radiance cold
Of that sweet soul that knows my own so well.

But look, my lips are parched with despair,
10 A thirsty fever does my eyes infest,
Sweet maiden, you, with long and golden hair.

But let your gentle breath my anguish wrest,
Your smile, with drunken joy, my soul ensnare;
Oh, end my pain at last . . . come to my breast.

SONNET

Without 'tis autumn, the wind beats on the pane
With heavy drops, the leaves high upwards sweep.
You take old letters from a crumpled heap,
And in one hour have lived your life again.

5   Musing, in this sweet wise the moments creep;
You pray no caller will your door attain;
Better it is when dreary falls the rain
To dream before the fire, awaiting sleep.

And thus alone, reclining in my chair,
10 The fairy Dochia's tale comes to my mind
While round me haze is gath'ring in the air.

Then softly down the passage footsteps wind,
Faint, sound of rustling silk upon the stair ...
And now my eyes cold, tapering fingers bind.

SONNET

The years have sped, and time still swiftly flies
Since that first sacred hour in which we met;
But how we loved I can no more forget,
Sweet wonder with cold hands and such big eyes.

5   O, come again! Your words inspire me yet,
While your soft gaze upon me gently lies,
That neath its ray new life in me shall rise,
And you new songs upon my lyre beget.

When you come near to me you little know
10 How soothed my heart is then, as though with balm,
As when some star does in the heavens show;

Your childish smile so full of tender charm
Has power to quench this life drawn out in woe
And fill my eyes with fire, my soul with calm.

SONNET

When e'en the inner voice of thought is still,
And does some sacred chant my soul endear,
'Tis then I call to thee; but will you hear?
Will from the floating mists your form distil?

5 Will night its tender power of wonder rear
And your great, peaceful eyes their light fulfill,
That of the rays that bygone hours spill
To me as in a dream you do appear?

But come to me ... come near, come still more near ...
10 Smiling you bend to gaze into my face
While does your sigh gentle love make clear.

Upon my eyes I feel your lashes' trace,
O love, for ever lost, for ever dear,
To know the aching thrill of your embrace!

SONNET

The years have passed like clouds across the dale;
The years have gone and will return no more,
For they no longer move me, as the lore
Of legend, and of song, and *doina's* tale

5   Brought wonder to my boyish brow of yore,
And mystery its meaning half unveil.
Your shade falls round me now to no avail,
O secret twilight hour on evening's shore.

To tear a sound out of the life that's gone,
10 To stir within my soul again its thrill
My hand upon the silent lyre is numb.

Ay, all is lost beneath youth's horizon,
The tender voice of bygone days is still,
While time rolls out behind me ... night has come.

SONNET

Mighty Venice now has fallen low,
One hears no songs, no sound of festive balls;
On steps of marble and through gateways falls
The pallid moon's unearthly silver glow.

5 Okeanos there his sorrow calls . . .
In *him* alone eternal youth does blow,
Yet on his bride would he his breath bestow;
The waves break plaintively against the walls.

The town is silent as a burial ground;
10 Only the priests of bygone days remain,
Saint Mark tolls sinister the midnight round;

In sombre tones his slow sibylline strain
He nightly speaks with smooth and cadenced sound;
« The dead, my child, no more come back again ».

LONGING

Come to the forest spring where wavelets
Trembling o'er the pebbles glide
And the drooping willow branches
Its secluded threshold hide.

5 Eagerly your arms outstretching,
Hurry dear to my embrace,
That the breeze your hair will gather
And uplift it from your face.

On my knees will you be seated
10 Just we two alone, alone,
While upon your curls disordered
Are the lime-tree's blossoms strown.

Forehead pale and tresses golden
On my shoulder you incline,
15 And your lip's delicious plunder
Raise up willingly to mine.

We will dream a dream of fairies
Rocked by secret lullaby,
Which the lovely spring is chanting
20 And the winds that wander by.

Midst that harmony thus sleeping
Woodland tales our thoughts enthrall,
And upon our bodies softly
Do the lime-tree petals fall.

MORTUA EST!

Two candles, tall sentry, beside an earth mound,
A dream with wings broken that trail to the ground,
Loud flung from the belfry calamitous chime ...
'Tis thus that you passed o'er the bound'ries of time.

5 Gone by are the hours when the heavens entire
Flowed rivers of milk and grew flowers of fire,
When the thunderous clouds were but castles erect
Which the moon like a queen each in turn did inspect.

I see you a shadow bright silver transcending,
10 With wings high uplifted to heaven ascending,
I see you slow climbing through the sky's scaffold bars
Midst a tempest of light and a snowstorm of stars;

While the witches the sound of their spinning prolong,
Exalted in sunshine, swept up by a song,
15 O'er your breast like a saint your white arms crossed in prayer,
And gold on the water, and silver in the air.

I see your soul's parting, its flight I behold;
Then gaze at the clay that remains ... mute and cold,
At the winding-sheet clung to the coffin's rude sill,
20 At your smile sweet and candid, that seems alive still.

And I ask times unending my soul torn with doubt,
O why, pallid angel, your light has gone out,
For were you not blameless and wonderfully fair?
Have you gone to rekindle a star in despair?

25 I fancy on high there are things without name,
Broad rivers of fire spanned by bridges of flame,
Strange castles that spires till the zenith up fling,
With stairways of incense and flowers that sing.

And you wander among them, a worshipful queen,
30 With hair of bright starlight and eyes vespertine,
In a tunic of turquoise bespattered with gold,
While a wreath of green laurels does your forehead enfold.

O, death is chaos, an ocean of stars gleaming,
While life is a quagmire of doubts and of dreaming.
35 Oh, death is an aeon of sun-blazoned spheres,
While life but a legend of wailing and tears.

Through my head beats a whirlwind, a clamorous wrangle
Of thoughts and of dreams that despair does entangle;
For when suns are extinguished and meteors fall
40 *The whole universe seems to mean nothing at all.*

Maybe that one day the arched heavens will sunder,
And down through their break all the emptiness thunder,
Void's night o'er the earth its vast nothing extending,
The loot of *an instant* of death *without ending.*

45 If so, then forever your flame did succumb,
And forever your voice from today will be dumb.
If so, the hereafter can bring no rebirth.
If so, then this angel was nothing but earth.

And thus, lovely soil that breath has departed,
50   I stand by your coffin alone broken-hearted;
And yet I don't weep, *rather* praise for its fleeing
Your ray softly crept from this chacs of being.

For who shall declare which is ill and which well,
The is, or the isn't? Can anyone tell?
55   For he who is not, even grief can't destroy,
And oft is the grieving, and seldom the joy.

To exist! O, what nonsense, what foolish conceit;
Our eyes but deceive us, our ears but cheat,
What this age discovers, the next will deny,
60   *Far better just nothing than naught but a lie.*

I see dreams in men's clothing that after dreams chase,
But that tumble in tombs ere the end of the race,
And I search in my soul how this horror to fly,
To laugh like a madman? To curse? Or to cry?

65   O, what is the meaning? What sense does agree?
The end of such beauty, had that got to be?
Sweet seraph of clay where still lingers life's smile,
Just in order to die did you live for a while?

O, tell me the meaning. This angel or clod?
70   I find on her forehead no witness of God.

EGYPT

Between far spreading Arab fields the Nile sweeps on its yellow way.
The fire and gold of Egypt skies unroll their splendour to the day,
Out of the deep slim rushes rise, fringing with green the flat
                                           brown marge;
Like heavenly gems the silent flowers glimmer and sparkle in the light,
5   Tender, tall and pure as snow some stand aloof and white,
Some fiery red, some blue like eyes that waste their sorrow's overcharge,

Among the weedy brakes that show wild in dense luxuriance, there
Are nests in which exotic birds display and preen their feather rare,
And lift their beaks in the sunlit air, and pour out sweet caressing song.
10 Drowned in its everlasting dreams, welling from sacred far off springs,
The Nile its silent legend and its restless yellow mirror swings
Towards the placid waiting sea, where does its soul at last belong.

Beside each bank green fertile plains in grateful smiling gladness lie.
On the horizon Memphis stands, a mighty mound against the *sky;*
15 Wall piled on wall, rock heaped on rock, a city raised by giant hands,
A thought fantastic built in stone, a human mind grown wondrous tall!
Like a mountain range in its ancient pride rise up the bastions of its wall
And clad by the day in a silver robe shine far across that prosperous land.

And it seems to rise from the glamour of dreams, from the empty
                                       wilderness of sleep,

20 From a hurricane of sand that the tempest's circling arm did reap;
    Like a thunderous thought of the holy sea flung by the sky to earth again.
    And there too rise from the trembling ground and stand in arrogant,
                                                    timeless pride
    The mighty pyramids of old, as strange and as strong as the death
                                                    they deride;
    Tombs which deep in their heavy breasts the epic of a scald contain.

25 Twilight falls . . . the Nile sleeps on and the stars rise secretly over
                                                    the sky,
    The moon on the sea her image throws, setting them midst the clouds
                                                    to fly.
    Who does the pyramid's door unclose? Who does across that threshold
                                                    climb?
    It is the lonely king, in a robe of scarlet embroidered with gems and
                                                    gold;
    'Tis he who enters the desert's tomb, and would the buried past unfold,
30 To break his heart in gazing back across the flooded ford of time.

    In vain the kings of the earth endeavour with justice and with strength
                                                    to reign,
    Rarer grow the deeds that prosper, omens ill around them gain.
    In vain indeed do they seek the reply to that riddle no man can tell.
    Night falls . . . and the shadows creep out of the desert's outmost places,
35 Across the Nile's long ebb, just as over the tides of stricken races,
    The brooding, lonely thoughts of that King like those deep shadows
                                                    darkening fell.

    The dream of the painted pyramids, of the cool flowing face of the Nile,
    The restless murmur of trembling reeds, beneath the moon's embracing
                                                    smile,
    That look like giant sheaves of corn, or an army of silver headed spears,
40 The hidden light of waters and all night and desert's greatness

63

Conspire to unfold beneath the moon that Empire's glory and timeless
night
And to conjure fantastic visions in air, and fill the deserts with strange
chimeres.
The sacred river whispers on in the rippling voice of the fleeting tide

The tale of its endless flowing by, of the nameless folk that have
lived by its side,
45 Till the soul is drunken with dreaming dreams as swift and as smooth
as the river's tale.
Endless groves of shivering palms, that gleam in the moonbeams' golden
light
And that lift their slender silver stems, like countless masts, to the
luminous night,
While the waves on the river delight in their spray and the sky on
its clouds sets sail.

In the stately ancient temples there, mid pillars of marble white as
snow,
50 Each night the Gods in their raiments pure with measured places come
and go,
While softly chanted to silver harps the songs of grey-haired priests arise.
To the endless sobbing winds of the sands, to the boundless dark of
the night around,
From the topmost stones of the pyramid's crest each night re-echoes
that ghostly sound
Of the Kings that moan in their mighty vaults, and fill the world's
dome with their sighs.

55 An Arab tower stands erect, the river flowing at its feet,
And there the magus gazes down upon that mirror's yellow sheet;
For all the sky with all its stars is faithfully assembled there,
And his own image very small seeks out amidst those tangled rays

64

The secret of eternity, till with a wand he draws the ways
60 That lead to what is right and true, and what is valuable and fair.

And thus perchance above the surge of a bloodless, pale and effeminate
folk,
Of villainous kings, debased with crime, of a priesthood concealed in
corruption's cloak,
The magus night's inverted sign will read that foretells of destruction
at last,
When the wind sweeps up from the desert's brow all its sand in a
mountain crested wave
65 That swallows tall cities with temple and tower, and makes of each
dwelling a grave,
Thus hiding the shame of a people defiled, of an era of darkness in
time that is past.

Hurricanes blindly gallop on, till their chargers finally fall in the race,
And the wind-lashed flood of the risen Nile sweeps frantically over
the desert's face,
That the best of Egypt's flowering plains are engulfed by the stream
in its raging strife.
70 And from Thebes to Memphis the country is turned to a ruined and
empty, desolate strand,
Where wandering tribes will plant their tents at night upon the
scorching sand,
A homeless people ranging wide through the lonely legend of their
life.

Once more the restless stars look down on the river's billowing mirror
of gold,
The red flamingo takes its way across the waters as of old,
75 O'er antique Egypt once again the silver moonlight palely laves.
And the soul turns back from its journeying dreams to listen anew to
the ancient story,

To the ears of the living present steals the wondrous pomp of the past
in its glory
While strange prophetic voices rise from the stirring muttering lips of
the waves.

Till Memphis lifts again its head above the desert's silver plan,
80 Shuddering still from the horrible shock of the tempest's blast of ruin
and pain . . .
And the Bedouin Arabs beneath the moon look up with awestruck
frightened eyes
And tell strange tales of flowers and stars that shine for an hour and
pass away,
Of cities that rise from the desert's bones and fade to dust at the close
of day,
And songs that out of the musical land and from under the sea at sunset
rise.

85 For bells there are beneath the sea, that muffled peal at evening hour,
And many a garden down in the Nile, with apple hanging orchard bower;
But under the silent desert sand a sad and stricken nation hides;
And when no one sees, these folk awake in their fallen cities that once
were strong.
And into the halls of Memphis proud as in the olden days they throng,
90 And drink and dance and make carouse, while the moon o'er the heavens
rides.

FAREWELL

We part for ever from today,
Farewell beloved one;
And I, unto may death, your way
                Will shun.

5   I care not now where you may go,
You can no more bereave me,
Today the sweetest girl I know
                Does leave me.

Nor shall I as in former hours
10 Build Spanish castles high,
With star-lit windows, and with towers
                Of sky,

When, shivering with bitter cold,
Through winter nights uncertain,
15 I watched lest you perhaps unfold
                Your curtain.

O what delight to stroll with you
Beneath the flowering plum-trees,
When poured its light their branches through,
20   The moon.

How often did I secret pray
Swift night her sails would furl,
That we might thus forever stray.
    Fair girl!

25 That I might catch with rapturous thrill
The words that you let fall,
And that today I barely still
    Recall.

For if today I part the veil
30 And see what time portended,
I feel that long ago the tale
    Was ended.

And when the moon enrapts the streams
And trembles on the fen,
35 A thousand years have flown it seems
    Since then.

For I no longer am confined
In that sweet country's spell;
Aye, I have left you far behind,
40   Farewell.

WHAT IS LOVE...

What is love? A lifetime spent
   Of days that pain does fill,
That thousand tears can't content,
   But asks for tears still.

5 With but a little glance coquet
   Your soul it knows to tie,
That of its spell you can't forget
   Until the day you die.

Upon your threshold does it stand,
10   In every nook conspire,
That you may whisper hand in hand
   Your tale of heart's aspire.

Till fades the very earth and sky,
   Your heart completely broken,
15 And all the world hangs on a sigh,
   A word but partly spoken.

It follows you for weeks and weeks
   And in your soul assembles
The memory of blushing cheeks
20   And eyelash fair that trembles.

It comes to you a sudden ray
    As though of starlight's spending,
How many and many a time each day
    And every night unending.

25 For of your life has fate decreed
    That pain shall it enfold,
As does the clinging water-weed
    About a swimmer hold.

THE FOREST POOL

Upon the forest pool's deep blue
Golden petalled lilies float;
Circling silver ripples play
Around an ancient rowing-boat.

5   I pass along the sloping bank,
I pause to listen, lost in dreams;
I see *Her* rise among the reeds,
She stretches out her arms it seems.

And hand-in-hand we leap aboard,
10 Charmed by the water's tiny childe;
The rudder strings slip from my grasp,
The oars into the water slide.

To float away wrapped in love
Beneath the kindly summer moon,
15 While midst the rushes breathes the wind
And endlessly the ripples croon.

But it is dream, she does not come,
And vainly do I moan and weep
Beside the dark blue forest pool
20 On which gold-petalled lilies sleep.

ANGEL AND DEMON

Blackness of the cathedral dome, saddened by the yellow light
Of waxen candles shimmering, which burn before the altars' face;
While in the dark and spacious vault, unpenetrated realms of space
Defy the tapers' tired eyes that strain to probe unconquered night.

5 And empty is the twilight church, save where, upon the marble stair,
A child who like an angel kneels with deeply bowed and fervent head.
Upon the altar stands, amidst the rosy light the tapers shed,
With calm, pale face and gentle mean an image of the virgin fair.

Within a sconce upon the wall a guttering candle burns and drips
10 And gleaming drops of molten pitch hiss as they fall upon the ground.
While wreaths of dry and withered flowers emit a gentle rustling sound.
And the maiden's secret prayer rests silently upon her lips.

Sunk in the outer ring of dark, a marble cross his form concealing,
Wrapped in the shadow's heavy cloak, *He* like a demon silent stands,
15 His elbows resting on the cross and hanging down his tapered hands,
His eyes deep sunken in his head, his furrowed brow strange grief
revealing.

Against the crosse's chilly neck his burning cheek he thoughtfully lays;
About its snowy arms is looped his long and raven hair.
The sad light of the candle glow scarce reaches to the corner where
20 Upon his drawn and pallid face fall feebly its yellow rays.

She ... an angel praying heaven — *He* ... a demon wrapped in woes'
She ... the pure, the golden hearted — *He* ... not heeding heaven's loss.
He ... in deathly shadow leaning on the cold arms of the cross —
While from the sad Madonna's feet *his* simple prayer to heaven goes.

25 Upon the wall by which she kneels, the high coal wall of marble fine
That shines as does the mountain snow, that as calm water turns the
                                                                 light,
Clearly as on a mirror falls the shadow of that maiden white,
Her bending shadow, like herself, kneeling in prayer before the shrine.

O what can ail thee, maiden sweet, with thy so gentle noble mien?
30 Pale is thy face as is the snow, and pale as wax thy tapered hands.
As river mist shot through with stars that on the hills at evening stands,
So shine thy innocent, soft eyes, beneath their veiling lashes seen.

Angel thou art, yet something lacks; an angel's tall, star-spattered wings.
But as I gaze I see take shape about your shoulders flying lines;
35 What are they, trembling in the air? Whence come these feathery designs?
An angel's pinion in the dusk towards the gate of heaven springs.

O, but the shadow is not hers; her guardian angel hovers there;
Against the whiteness of the wall I see his radiant figure tower.
Over the maiden's sinless life he watches with celestial power,
40 And as she bows her head to pray, he too is bowed in fervent prayer.

But if this be an angel's wing, then *She* too angel is; for though
The airy brightness of her wings is not revealed to eyes of man,
These walls alone, where age long prayer has been poured out in worship,
                                                                 can
Proclaim to us her angelhood and of her wings existence show.

73

45 I love, I love thee fain would cry the demon from the twilight shade,
But the winged shadow guarding her the utterance of his spirit sealed.
The passion died upon his lips; in worship not in love he kneeled
And heard across the hollow nave her timid murmur as she prayed.

. . . .

She? A princess fair as day, a crown of stars upon her head,
50 An angel in a woman's guise, going her happy way through life.
He? A rebel of mankind, blowing to flame the sparks of strife
And sowing hate in hopeless breasts that to revolt by him are led.

Their ways of life are worlds apart, deep oceans lie between these twain,
Between them barricades of thought, the bitter bloodshed of a race.
55 And yet at times their journeys cross, they meet each other face to face,
Their eyes seek out each other's soul and mingle with a curious pain.

With gentle yet absorbing gaze, her large and starlike deep blue eyes
Rest thoughtfully on his that do the tempest and the lightning show.
While on his pallid face there mount emotions warm and tender glow.
60 They love . . . and yet what worlds apart, what universe between them
lies.

A monarch pale has come from far, a time old crown he humbly brings;
The victor in a hundred wars, his conquests would he make her own.
He begs to lead her as his bride along the carpet to his throne
And place within her tiny hand the sceptre of the king of kings.

65 But no, with parted lips she turns and does not speak the fatal word;
Her heart is silent in her breast and from the king she draws her hands,
Her virgin soul is filled with love, while in her dreams there ever stands
The demon's image like a god, for every night his voice she heard.

74

She seems to see him leading men with words of fire, with
winged ideas;
70 How brave, how powerful, how grand — she thought in lovers' proud
delight;
He leading on the rising age to conquer and to claim its right
Against the lifeless piled up weight of wisdom that experience rears.

She saw him standing on a rock, wrapt like a garment with his wrath
As with his banner's scarlet folds; his beetling forehead deeply scoured
75 As though a black tempestuous night when all the host of hell's aboard.
Out of his eyes the lightning gleamed, intoxicating words poured forth.

. . . .

On a bed of boards the young man lies stretched in the agony of death,
Beside his couch a dim lamp burns, its poor thin wick and meagre flame
Struggle against the cold damp air. No man has ever heard his name,
80 None comes to ease his bitter lot, or wet his lips that choke for breath.

O past are the days when in the world the thunder of his voice
would roll
Against the written codes of law, against the laws that bound
and maimed,
And slew men in the name of God . . . today the world's revenge is
aimed
Upon the dying heretic, and stifles out his stricken soul.

85 To die bereft of every hope, what man is there on earth who knows
The awful meaning of these words? To feel enslaved and weak
and small,
To fight and hope and see your plans shrivelled to nothing after all,
To know that in the world is throned an evil force none may oppose.

Your years were spent in strife with wrong, and you a useless fight
                                              have fought,
90 And now you die and see your life was wrecked in work *without a vail*,
Such death is Hell. More bitter tears than these ne'er coursed the
                                                    visage pale
Of dying man. How cruel *to know that you* and all the world *are naught*.

Such black thoughts rising in his soul delay the death for which
                                              he yearns.
With what great gifts has he been born. What passionate love of
                                              right and truth,
95 What sympathy for human kind, and all the lofty flame of youth.
Behold his recompense at last, this agony with which he burns.

But into that narrow tawdry room, breaking the mist that veiled
                                              his eye,
A silver shadow softly creeps; behold, an angel shape comes near,
Sits lightly on the wretched bed, kisses away each blinding tear
100 From those dimmed eyes; and now the mist is torn away in ecstasy.

Aye, it is *She*. And with what joy, joy fathomless, before unknown,
He gazes in his angel's face and reads love's tender pity there.
With long glance he is repaid all his life's anguish and despair.
He whispers with dis dying breath: "My love I know thee for my own.

105 I who have laboured all my life poor and helpless souls to move,
Warring against the open skies with all my burning discontent;
A demon, yet not cursed by God, for in my dying hour he sent
His angel here to give me peace, and of his peace the name is love."

76

BLUE FLOWER

« You ride the clouds and range the sky
Your net about the stars cast;
But do remember dear at last
My soul can never soar so high.

5 You build tall palaces in Spain
Of fancy's fragile masonry,
You search in vain the sullen sea
And roam Assyria's plains in vain.

The pyramids their summits press
10 Against the clouded heavens high,
Dear heart, it is not wise to fly
Too far afield for happiness ! »

T'was thus she spoke in whispers low,
Her hand laid softly on my head,
15 But I just laughed and nothing said,
Yet what she told was truth, I know.

« Come where cool crystal brooks complain
Their fleeting fate midst forest greens,
And where the hanging cliff out leans
20 As though to thunder on the plain.

And somewhere, up some little glade,
To gather raspberries we will climb,
Or sit and watch the sky sublime
From neath the rushes' tasseled shade.

25 While many a story you will tell,
And many a lie you'll whisper too;
But I will read on petals true
You love me not, you love me well.

As rosy as an apple's rind
30 Will be my cheeks burnt by the sun,
And my long golden hair undone
Around your neck in coils you'll wind.

While if your lips on mine should burn
No one in all the world will know,
35 My hat is broad ... and even so,
'Twere only your and my concern.

And when the moon comes shining through
The gap where tangled branches part,
You'll hold me very close, dear heart,
40 And I will clasp my arms round you.

And when we walk the twilight gloom
Of forest paths that homeward run,
We'll gather many a kiss, each one
As fragrant as the violets' bloom.

45 And long amid the starlight glow
We'll stand to talk outside my gate,
For no one comes that way so late,
And who should care I love you so?»

Another kiss and she was gone;
50 Like post I stood in the moon's stream!
O beautiful beyond a dream,
O small blue flower all my own!

· ·

Alas our love that grew so fair
Has flown and faded from that hour,
55 O my blue flower, my blue flower! . . .
The world is sorrow everywhere.

THE BRAZEN BELLS OF MIDNIGHT...

The brazen bells of midnight upon the darkness toll,
But sleep, life's custom agent, won't take from me his dole;
Down paths so many follow, death would my spirit lead,
And death, when all considered, resembles life indeed;
5 While in my heart the balance does level stand between
And neither to the one, nor to the other lean.

GUARDIAN ANGEL

When my soul lay awake late last night, did it seem
That I saw my good angel come down as in a dream,
Engirdled with moonlight and silver star gleam,
And hover above me with wings wide outspread.
5   But you, when he spied, in your snowy white dress,
O child of sweet wonder, and secret caress,
Quite awed and astonished my guardian fled.

Good child, are you demon that just at one glance
Of your eyes through their lashes thrown softly askance
10 My angel and friend left his long vigilance?
O guardian angel, come back, do not flee
For this girl...! But no, let your long lashes fall,
That your pale lovely features again I recall,
               For you... *you are he.*

SO DELICATE

So delicate, so pure you are
As April's snow-white cherry bloom;
An angel come to earth, a star
That does within my chamber loom.

5   The silken carpet at your tread
Whispers softly, and you seem,
From tiny foot to high poised head,
To float as lightly as a dream.

Amidst your mantle's hanging folds
10 Your limbs like burning marble glow.
Your magic all my spirit holds,
Your eyes that brim both joy and woe.

Your beauty like a dream beguiles,
Fair as a bride's in legends old;
15 Smile not, dear heart, because your smiles
Are beauty in your face retold.

How surely neath the cloak of night
Could you destroy me with your charms,
A burning word of love's delight,
20 A single clasp of your cold arms.

And now a .veil of meditation
Creeps, and clouds your eyes' deep fire;
The shadow of renunciation,
The shade of sweet, unquenched desire.

25 You go, I understand too well
To try to keep you by my side;
For me forever lost, farewell,
O strange and lovely legend's bride!

To gaze on you itself was wrong,
30 How can I ever make amends,
Save by lamenting all life long
The happiness that this day ends.

As Mary's icon now you glow
With holy light that cannot wane
35 Wearing a halo on your brow.
O come to me, come back again!

O MOTHER...

O mother, darling mother, lost in time's formless haze
Amidst the leaves' sweet rustle you call my name always;
Amidst their fluttering murmur above your sacred grave
I hear you softly whisper whene'er the branches wave;
5 While o'er your tomb the willows their autumn raiment heap ..
For ever wave the branches, and you for ever sleep.

When I shall die, beloved, do not beside me mourn,
But break a branch of blossom that does the lime adorn,
And take it very softly, and plant it at my head;
10 I'll feel its shadow growing as on the soil it's shed;
And watered by the tears that you for sorrow weep...
For ever grow that shadow, and I for ever sleep.

And should it be together that we shall die one day,
They shall not in some cemet'ry our separate bodies lay,
15 But let them dig a grave near where the river flows
And in a single coffin them both together close;
That I to time eternal my love beside me keep...
For ever wail the water, and we for ever sleep.

WITH LIFE'S TOMORROW TIME YOU GRASP

With life's tomorrow time you grasp,
Its yesterdays you fling away,
And still, in spite of all remains
Its long eternity, today.

5   When one thing goes, another comes
In this wide world by heaven borne;
And when the sun is setting here
'Tis somewhere else just breaking dawn.

It seems somehow that other waves
10 Are rolling down the same old stream,
And somehow, though the autumns change,
'Tis but the same leaves fall it seem.

Before our night does ever ride
The queen of mornings rosy skies;
15 While even death is but a guess,
Of life a notion, a surmise.

Of every moment that goes by
One fact each mortal creature knows;
The universe is poised in time
20 And whirling round for ever goes.

Still, though this year will fly away
And soon but to the bygone add,
Within your soul you ever hold
Each thing of worth you ever had.

25   With life's tomorrow time you grasp,
Its yesterdays you fling away,
And still, in spite of all remains
Its long eternity, today.

A radiant and brilliant view,
30   In many rapid glimpses caught,
Of infinite, unending calm,
Bathed in the rays of timeless thought.

THE WAVES OF TIME

Arise again, beloved, out of the waves of time
With your long golden tresses and marble arms sublime;
Your face that now tranparent and pale as wax is pale
Is shaded by the shadow of sorrow's clinging veil!
5   Your timid smile caressing does rest within my eyes,
O star amidst fair women, o queen of starry skies;
Your head upon your shoulder its wealth of beauty lays
And in your eyes of wonder I'm lost and weeping gaze.

Out of the void's dark vapours may you once more uprear,
10 That to my heart I clasp you, beloved angel dear,
That I in nameless weeping above your face may bend
And on your lips forever my burning kisses spend.
While your cold hand unheeding I clasp against my breast,
Closer, yet still closer, against my bosom pressed.

15 Alas, not thus the darkness gives back its own again;
Now through its icy vapours I see your shadow wane.
With hanging arms and helpless once more I am alone
Before a dream unending of hours that have gone;
In vain with arms outstretching my soul your shadow craves,
20 Dear one, I cannot reach you amidst time's rolling waves.

THE TALE OF THE FOREST

Mighty emperor is the forest,
High dominion does he wield,
And a thousand races prosper
'Neath the shelter of his shield.

5　The moon, the sun and Lucifer
Do round his kingdom ever sphere;
While lords and ladies of his court
Are of the noble race of deer.

Hares, his heralds and his postmen,
10　Carry rapidly his mails;
Birds his orchestra composing
Springs that tell him thousand tales.

Midst the flowers that grow in shadow.
By the streams and in the grass,
15　Bees in golden clouds are swarming,
Ants in mighty armies pass . . .

Come, let us again be children
In the woods we loved of yore
So that life, and luck, and loving
20　Seem a game and nothing more.

For I feel that mother nature
All her wisdom did employ
But to raise you over living
And of life to make your toy.

25 You and I away shall wander
Quite alone where no one goes,
And we'll lie beside the water
Where the flowering lime-tree grows.

As we slumber, on our bodies
30 Will the lime its petals lay,
While in sleep, sweet distant bagpipes
We will hear some shepherd play.

Hear so much, and closer clinging,
Heart to heart in lovers' wise,
35 Hear the emperor call his council
And his ministers advise.

Through the silver spreading branches
Will the moon the stream enlace,
And around us slowly gather
40 Courtiers of many a race.

Horses proud, as white as wave crests,
Many-branching horned stags,
Bulls with stars upon their foreheads,
Chamois from the mountain crags.

45 And the lime-tree they will question
Who we are; and stand and wonder,
While our host will softly answer
Parting wide his boughs asunder:

« Look, o look how they are dreaming
50   Dreams that in the forest grow;
Like the children of some legend
Do they love each other so ».

EMPEROR AND PROLETARIAN

Squatting on wooden benches, within a tavern bare,
Where daylight's rays but dimly through dirty windows show,
Before a long, stained table, their faces drawn with care,
Wearied out by wandering and doubting's black despair,
5 These are the wretched sons of poverty and woe.

"Ah friends," said one, "you think man is a light that glows
Upon this earth of sorrowing and misery?
Why, not a spark is there in him that candid shows;
His lamp is dark as is this globe on which he grows,
10 And over which the lord omnipotent is he.

Tell me then what justice means ... The powerful secure
Behind their wealth, within their circling laws conspire
To mass still greater wealth against the needy poor,
Against ourselves; that we shall all the toil endure
15 Bowed down and bent in labour's yoke our lives entire.

Some pass their time in ceaseless revelry and play;
The hours smile for them, and amber wine they drink;
The winter months in gardens do they wile away,
Coolness of alpine snows the summer fires allay;
20 They turn the morn to eve, and from the sun's eye shrink.

Virtue for them does not exist, but they will preach
Sacrificing, love and diligence to us.
The heavy car of state must rumble on, and each
Of you must pour his blood into the battle's breach,
25 That of *your* endless pain *they* may grow prosperous.

Countless, mighty hosts, and navies on the sea,
Splendid golden crowns on noble foreheads worn,
Riches from near and far, in thoughtless quantity,
These hold the rich aloft in high sublimity;
30 While on our aching backs are all the burdens born.

Religion — but a tale, astutely spread abroad
To rivet on your shoulders the heavy harnessed load,
For, had you lost all hope of heavenly reward
After a life on earth with pain and hardship scored,
35 Would you go on working as an ox beneath the goad?

With what strange phantom shadows are your illusions fed
That make you set your faith in heaven's promised store?
No, when your life is passed, all hope of joy is sped,
And he who dies in misery, in misery is dead;
40 For those who pass the grave come back again no more.

In lies and windy phrases their state and safety stands,
Their holy law and order is but an empty creed;
To keep their stolen wealth safe from your needy hands,
They arm you to destroy your like on foreign lands,
45 And you against yourselves triumphantly they lead.

Why should you be slaves of their immoral gold,
You who scarcely live for all your endless toil?
Why should disease and death you in their arms enfold,
While they in plenitude and boundless wealth grow old
50 Even as though they hoped to cheat death of its spoil?

How do you forget the power that numbers mean?
You could take back today your rights they will not give.
Build no more these walls with which their wealth they screen,
Or which for prisons serve when pressed by torments keen
55 You dare assert at last the right you have to live.

Every pleasure they enjoy surrounded by their law
And all their careless days in utmost sweetness spend,
In luxury and vice, and drunken wild uproar.
They call your virgins in, blind instruments before
60 Their old corrupted satyrs who their young beauty rend.

And should you ask yourselves what part is left for you:
The drudgery on which is based their happiness,
A lifelong servitude, and crumbs of bread a few.
Robbed of your daughters, and dishonoured too . . .
65 For them the earth and sky, for you naught but distress.

They have no need of rules: virtue is easy when
All that you want you have. Round *you* their laws are wound,
Their punishments designed to strike you, wretched men
Who date to stretch a hand to ask your own again:
70 Even your needs become a crime that has no bound.

Hurl to the earth their scheme founded on greed and wrong.
This system that divides, making us rich and poor!
Since there will be no prize in death awaited long,
Demand the rights today that do to you belong,
75 And let us live in equal brotherhood secure!

Smash down the antique bronze that Venus naked shows;
Let pictures that do wickedly entice be brought to dust,
Snowy limbs that tell of wonders no man knows,
And break in passions rude our maidens soft repose,
80 And lead them unawares into the claws of lust!

Scatter wide what rouses and sustains perverted mind,
Temple and palace storm that shield disgrace and crime,
Melt the statues tall that of tyranny remind;
Wash from the marble steps the footprints left behind
85 By those who near the great through lies and pandering climb !

Banish the signs of pomp and false deceiving pride;
O, strip from daily life the granite robe it wears,
Its purple and its gold . . . its foul and ugly hide;
To make of life a dream, of living purified,
90 That without passion is and happiness prepares.

Gigantic pyramids from this life's ruins raise,
A *memento mori* unto the end of time;
To open out our souls that we may justice praise
Unto eternity, not nude and shameful ways,
95 With harlot soul, and eyes grown wild with lust and crime.

Oh, let the deluge loose; you've waited long to know
What recompense your meek humility will get;
The wolf and the hyena do in the courtiers grow,
Their cruelties of old still baser patterns show,
100 Only the form is changed, the evil lives on yet.

Strike and the golden era will return to us again,
Of which old legends tell us that all was gay and fair;
That happiness in life be equal for all men.
Even the touch of death will not be awful then,
105 But seem a smiling angel with long and golden hair.

Then you will die contented and not by sorrow wrung,
Your children will be born and in full gladness live.
Even the church will not bewail with iron tongue
The passing of the free to live the blest among:
110 None will lament the dead who took all life could give.

Thus slowly will grow less the toll of dire disease,
While that alone will flourish which nature did intend,
And all these things will come in gradual degrees,
Till man but leaves the earth when earth no more can please.
115 The brimming cup of life drained empty to the end."

. . . .

Along the banks of Seine, drawn in a gala coach
The great king slowly goes, pallid and deep in thought.
Neither the lapping waves, nor rumbling wheels encroach
Upon his brooding mind; before his train's approach
120 There stands the suffering crowd with suffering distraught.

With ready piercing glance, and subtle smiling air,
He reads the secret thought that fills the people's soul,
The hand that holds the fate of those poor creatures there
Salutes them now with bland, acutely reasoned care
125 *Because his fate and theirs is but one single whole.*

Loveless he is, and lone, going so grandly by;
Convinced like all of you that malice, vice and hate
Will always govern all things and under all things lie,
While ever human history its age-old course will ply
130 As on time's heavy anvil blind hammers heedless fate.

So he whose very person is tyranny's high crest
Nods a gentle greeting to these ragged human things.
If they who are the power on which his glories rest
Would one day raise their heads or challenge his behest,
135 Low, yes low indeed, would fall the king of kings.

For all your shrewd mistrust, your deeply doubting sense,
Your cold and bitter smile that ne'er to pity woke,
For all your strong belief that law is but pretence,

For all your numbers might, the shade of violence,
140 'Tis he who holds you dumbly, still toiling in the yoke.

· ·

Paris is drowned in fire; the tempest bathes in flame,
Steeples like black torches blaze in the wind away.
Amidst the billowing sea whose waves no power could tame,
Cries and the clash of arms high battle do acclaim.
145 In very truth in France an age has died today.

Down streets where flaming houses glitter on pikes and sword
Barricades arise from blocks of granite piled;
An army marching forwards, the proletarian horde,
Company on company, that soon the ramparts board
150 Midst thunderous echoing clang of the alarm bells wild.

With faces pale as marble, as marble too as cold,
Women carrying muskets pass through the ruddy glow.
Their hair hangs o'er their shoulders and does their breasts enfold;
Mad with lifelong suffering and with dark hatred bold,
155 Black their eyes, yet gleaming with the brightness of despair.

Courage little soldiers wrapped in your tresses long,
Great today has grown the poor abandoned child,
Through the fire and ashes to justice march along,
For all your deeds of horror do to this hour belong;
160 Not you to blame, but those who your young souls defiled!

· ·

And now the ocean shines, as though were on it laid
And slid upon themselves broad plates of crystal bright;
While low above the trees, the secret forest glade,
The lonely yellow moon on azure field displayed
165 O'erfloods the silent world with her triumphal light.

Across the silver swell, with motion smooth and slow
Ocean battered ships draw their old wooden sides;
Like mighty gliding shadows across the sea they go,
While through their straining canvass the moonbeams seem to
                                                    throw
170   A fiery golden wheel that e'er before them rides.

Upon a cliff corroded by the billows' restless chide,
Beneath a weeping willow, with branches to the ground,
The king of kings is gazing out o'er the falling tide
Where gleaming silver circles midst one another glide,
175   And where the night breeze wanders with slow and cadenced sound.

And to the king it seemed that through the starlight fair,
Treading the forest trees, and crossing the ocean clear,
With long and snowy beard, and heavy thoughtful air,
A crown of withered grasses caught to his tangled hair
180   There came the mad King Lear.

With mute astonishment he watched that shadow hang
Against the riven clouds, through which the stars unfurled
Blazed out; and in his head a train of visions sprang . . .
Till loudly echoing above it all there rang
185   The people's voices that clothed in fire the stricken world:

"In every man the earth is entirely built once more.
Old Demiurgos still strives within each heart in vain,
For every mind puts in questions that all have put before:
Why is the flower that blooms to death inheritor?
190   Longings strange and sad, that rise in obscure pain.

The seed of a whole world of greatness and desire
At hazard have been sown within the hearts of all;
And when their time is come, their nature does aspire

After a perfect fruit, with all its strength entire;
195 Yet ere the fruit be ripe, the blossoms often fall.

Thus is the human fruit oft frozen in the bloom;
One man becomes a king, another but a slave,
Covering with chaos their different lots too soon,
Before the morning sun their works like petals strewn;
200 Yet nature to them all an equal knowledge gave.

Throughout the length of time, different and still the same
Their yearnings and their hopes are of one kind composed,
And though of countless fashions does seem life's secret flame,
All are alike deceived that call upon her name;
205 While infinite desire is in an atom closed.

When you but recollect that death will end this dream,
That nothing much is changed the day your life is passed,
This struggling desire to right the world will seem
Folly, and you'll grow tired; but one thing true you'll deem:
210 *That life is but the way to endless death at last.*

DOWN WHERE THE LONELY POPLARS GROW

Down where the lonely poplars grow
    How often have I erred;
My steps that all the neighbours know
    You only have not heard.

5 Towards your window lighted through
    How oft my gaze has flown;
A world entire my secret knew
    You only have not known.

A word, a murmur of reply
10   How often did I pray!
What matters then if I should die,
    Enough to live that day;

To know one hour of tenderness,
    One hour of lovers' night;
15 To hear your whisper's soft caress
    One hour, then come what might!

Had you but granted me a glance
    That was not filled with scorn,
Out of its shining radiance
20   A new star had been born.

You would have lived through lives untold
    Beyond the ends of time;
O deity with arms so cold,
    O marble form sublime!

25 An idol of some pagan lore
    As now no more is seen,
Come down to us from times of yore,
    From times that long have been.

My worship was of ages gone,
30   Sad eyes by faith beguiled,
Each generation handed on
    From father unto child.

But now I very little care
    To walk along that lane,
35 Nor heed the face I found so fair
    Looks out for me in vain;

For you are like them all today
    In bearing and in guise,
And I but look on your display
40   With cold and lifeless eyes.

You should have known to value right
    With wondering intent,
And lit your *candela* at night
    To Love that God had sent.

GLOSS

Days go past and days come still,
All is old and all is new,
What is well and what is ill,
You imagine and construe
5 *Do not hope and do not fear,*
Waves that leap like waves must fall;
Should they praise or should they jeer,
Look but coldly on it all.

Things you'll meet of many a kind,
10 Sights and sounds, and tales no end,
But to keep them all in mind
Who would bother to attend?...
Very little does it matter,
If you can yourself fulfil,
15 That with idle, empty chatter
Days go past and days come still.

Little heed the lofty ranging
That cold logic does display
To explain the endless changing
20 Of this pageantry of joy,
And which out of death is growing
But to last an hour or two;
For the mind profoundly knowing
All is old and all is new.

25 As before some troup of actors,
    You before the world remain;
    Act they Gods, or malefactors,
    'Tis but they dressed up again.
    And their loving and their slaying,
30 Sit apart and watch, until
    You will see behind their playing
    What is well and what is ill.

    What has been and what to be
    Are but of a page each part
35 Which the world to read is free.
    Yet who knows them off by heart?
    All that was and is to come
    Prospers in the present too,
    But its narrow modicum
40 *You imagine and construe.*

    With the selfsame scales and gauges
    This great universe to weigh,
    Man has been for thousand ages
    Sometimes sad and sometimes gay;
45 Other masks, the same old story,
    Players pass and reappear,
    Broken promises of glory;
    Do not hope and do not fear.

    Do not hope when greed is staring
50 O'er the bridge that luck has flung,
    These are fools for not despairing,
    On their brows though stars are hung;
    Do not fear if one or other
    Does his comrades deep enthrall,
55 Do not let him call you brother,
    Waves that leap like waves must fall.

Like the sirens' silver singing
Men spread nets to catch their prey,
Up and down the curtain swinging
60 Midst a whirlwind of display.
Leave them room without resistance,
Nor their commentaries cheer,
Hearing only from a distance,
Should they praise or should they jeer.

65 If they touch you, do not tarry,
Should they curse you, hold your tongue,
All your counsel must miscarry
Knowing who you are among.
Let them muse and let them mingle,
70 Let them pass both great and small;
Unattached and calm and single,
Look but coldly on it all.

Look but coldly on it all,
Should they praise or should they jeer;
75 *Waves that leap like waves must fall,*
Do not hope and do not fear.
You imagine and construe
What is well and what is ill;
All is old and all is new,
80 *Days go past and days come still.*

FAIR LOVE, OUR MUTUAL FRIEND

Fair love, our mutual friend, took wing,
    That is the reason why
My melancholy song must sing
    To all the world goodby.

5 Frail memory's cold finger tips
    Will shut the past away,
That it no more shall cross my lips,
    Nor through my spirit stray.

How many a murmuring of streams,
10   How many starlit flowers,
How many, many lover's dreams
    I've buried with the hours.

To what unfathomed depth unknown
    Had they their roots in me;
15 And, wetted by my tears, have grown,
    Beloved one, for thee.

Through what sad torment did they rear,
    Their blossoms to fulfill;
And, oh, how sorry am I, dear,
20   That I don't suffer still.

But you are now for ever gone,
Death called you very far;
And those gay eyes that glory shone
Now full of darkness are.

25 Your wistfully enchanted smile
Did somehow know, it seem,
To make of dream real life a while,
And out of life a dream.

And now I feel that you must dwell
30   Where the moon brightly lights
That country which the legends tell
Of thousand and one nights.

Love's mystery was too complete,
Too gentle and too strong;
35 A dream too wonderfully sweet
That it could last for long.

Maybe too much an angel you,
Too little just a girl,
That this strange ecstasy we knew
40   Its wings so soon should furl.

Too much dear one both you and I
In love's embrace were blind;
Too much forgot the lord on high;
Too much forgot mankind.

45 Maybe indeed there is no room
In a world filled with distress,
Midst so much grief, and so much gloom,
For so much happiness.

THE MURMUR OF THE FOREST

On the pond bright sparks are falling,
Wavelets in the sunlight glisten;
Gazing on the woods with rapture,
Do I let my spirit capture
5 Drowsiness, and lie and listen . . .
                Quails are calling.

All the silent water sleeping
Of the streams and of the rivers;
Only where the sun is shining
10 Thousand circles there designing
As with fright its surface shivers,
                Swiftly leaping.

Pipe the birds midst woods concealing,
Which of us their language guessing?
15 Birds of endless kinds and races
Chirp amidst its leafy places
And what wisdom they expressing
                And what feeling.

Asks the cuckoo: "Who has seen
20 Our beloved summer idol,
Beautiful beyond all praising
Through her languid lashes gazing,

Our most lovely, tender, bridal,
               Forest queen?"

25 Bends the lime with gentle care
Her sweet body to embower;
In the breeze his branches singing
Lift her in their arms upswinging,
While a hundred blossoms shower
30   On her hair.

Asks the brooklet as it flows
"Where has gone my lovely lady?
She, who evening hour beguiling,
In my silver surface smiling,
35 Broke its mirror deep and shady
               With her toes?"

I replied: "O forest, she
Comes no more, no more returning!
Only you, great oaks, still dreaming
40 Violet eyes, like flowers gleaming,
That the summer through were yearning
               Just for me."

Happy then, alone we twain,
Through the forest brush-wood striding!
45 Sweet enchanted tale of wonder
That the darkness broke asunder ...
Dear, wherever you'd be hiding,
               Come again!

Although the world would call me free
Each year the more her slave am I,
For in her very way to be
There's I don't know what, I don't know why.

5 Already from the day we met
Was my freedom mortal shot?
She's but a girl as they, and yet
There's something more, I don't know what.

No matter what we speak, or do,
10 The moments in sweet silence fly,
For somehow there is music too
When she is mute, I don't know why.

So likely to my dying day
To follow her will be my lot,
15 For in her sweet and candid way
There's I don't know why, I don't know what.

YOU GO...

You go, and years of pain untold,
O being that I dearly love,
My eyes will nevermore behold
The way you smile, the way you move.

5 And it is not as legend kind,
This love of mine torn by despair,
A demon does your soul confine
Sweet maid with face as marble fair.

Your forehead's pale enchanted spell,
10 Your eyes that sparkling brilliance store,
So humid, yet so fierce and fell,
That mischief gleam and yet implore.

I tremble when I feel you near,
I start whene'er I hear your stride,
15 And to your curving eyelash, dear,
My whole existence has been tied.

You go, nor do I greatly care
The ending of our yesterday,
For was there aught but torment there,
20 And suffering without allay?

No more your breath will softly chide
My ears with sweet and tender thrall;
Nor o'er my brow your fingers glide
Until I loose my senses all.

25   I could have coined in my mind
Defamatory names to dub you,
And I was fiercely hating you,
And cursing you, because I love you.

For now e'en that has passed away,
30   I have naught but my souvenirs;
Tomorrow will be as today,
And as tomorrow all the years.

Fair autumn still its breeze delays
Upon the springs that wail and sigh,
35   And through the leaves the whisper strays
Of my sad dreams that now must die.

My life a madness seems to be,
Ere it began was it dispelled;
In all this black eternity,
40   Your beauty scarce one moment held.

Since then my happiness has flown,
My luck for evermore has set.
Give back that moment's joy I've known,
With all its years of long regret.

O'ER THE WOODS

O'er the woods the moon's afloat,
Leaves move softly in the breeze,
Midst the branching alder trees
Sounds the horn its plaintive note.

5 Farther through the forest deep,
Farther yet, and yet more faint,
Blows again its sweet complaint,
Promise of eternal sleep.

While my heart to you is born
10 Why does fade away your sound?
Will you once for me resound
Melancholy hunter's horn?

DROWSY BIRDS

Drowsy birds at even gliding,
Round about their nests alight,
In among the branches hiding...
                    Dear, good night!

5 Silence through the forest creeping,
Lullaby the river sighs;
In the garden flowers sleeping...
                    Shut your eyes!

Glides the swan among the rushes
10 To its rest where moonlight gleams,
And the angels' whisper hushes...
                    Peaceful drems!

O'er the sky stars without number,
On the earth a silver light,;
15 All is harmony and slumber...
                    Dear, good night!

RETURN

(in the folk style)

"Forest, trusted friend and true,
Forest dear, how do you do?
Since the day I saw you last
Many, many years have passed
5 And though you still steadfast stand
I have travelled many a land."

"Yea, and I, what have I done?
Watched the years their seasons run;
Heard the squalls that through me groan
10 Ere my singing birds have flown;
Heard the creaking of my boughs
Neath the mounted winter snows.
Yea indeed, what have I done?
Done as I have always done;
15 Felt my summer leaves re-growing,
Heard the village girls who going
By the path that meets the spring
Melancholy *doina* sing".

"Forest, though the tempests blow,
20 The years come and the years go.
And the seasons wax and wane,
You are ever young again".

"What of seasons, when for ages
All the sky my lake engages;
25   What of years ill or good,
When the sap mounts in the wood;
What of years good or ill,
When the Danube rolls on still.
Only man is always changing,
30   O'er the world forever ranging;
We each do our place retain,
As we were, so we remain;
Oceans, rivers, mountains high
And the stars that light the sky,
35   Saturn with its whirling rings,
And the forest with its springs".

WHEN MEMORY...

When memory of bygone days
   My spirit would detain,
Down long and often trodden ways
   I travel the past again.

5 Above your house are lit as then
   The same bright stars of old.
That shone those summer evenings when
   My passion's tale I told.

And through the branches' silver lace
10   The moon peers from above,
As when midst lovers' warm embrace
   We whispered of our love.

Our hearts a solemn vow then took
   To love for ever and aye;
15 While tenderly the lilac shook
   Its blossoms on our way.

Could ever such a love as ours
   In night's oblivion wane,
While still among the thirsty flowers
20   The bubbling springs complain;

While still above the woods asleep
    The moon her journey plies;
While still your lips their beauty keep
    And coaxing are your eyes?

DOINA

From Tisa to the Nistru's tide
All Roumania's people cried
That they could no longer stir
For the rabbled foreigner.
5 From Hotin down to the sea
Rides the Muscal cavalry;
From the sea back to Hotin
Nothing but their host is seen;
While from Dorna to Boian
10 Seems the plague has spread its ban;
Leaving on our land a scar
That you scarcely know it more.
Up the mountains down the dale,
Have our foes flung far their trail.
15 From Sacele to Satmar
Only foreign lords there are;
While Roumanians one and all
Like the crab must backwards crawl.
And reversed is everything:
20 Spring for them is no more spring,
Summer is no longer summer,
They, at home, the foreign comer.
From Turnu up to Dorohoi
Does the alien horde deploy
25 And our fertile fields enjoy.
With their rumbling trains they come

Making all our voices dumb,
And our birds so much affray
That in haste they fly away.
30 Nothing now but withered thorn
Does the Christian's hearth adorn.
And the smiling earth they smother;
Forest — good Roumanian brother —
You too bend before their tide,
35 And the very springs they've dried.
Sad is this our countryside.

Who has sent them to these parts,
May the dogs eat out their hearts;
May the night their homes efface,
40 And with them this shameless race.

Stephen, mighty emperor,
You in Putna reign no more,
While his holy Prelacy
Guards alone the monastery,
45 Where the priests in fervent prayer
Of the saints take pious care.
Let them toll the bells away,
All the night and all the day,
And the gracious Lord invoke
50 That he come and save your folk!
Stephen rise up from the ground,
And your battle trumpet sound
All Moldavia gathered round.
Blow your trumpet just one blare,
55 All Moldavia will be there;
Let your trumpet blazen two
That the forests follow you;
Let your trumpet blazen three,

That our foes demolished be
60 From the mountains to the sea,
That the crows may hear their knell
And the gallows-tree as well.

ONE WISH ALONE HAVE I

One wish alone have I :
    In some calm land
Beside the sea to die;
    Upon its strand
5 That I forever sleep,
    The forest near,
    A heaven near,
Stretched o'er the peaceful deep.
    No candles shine,
10 Nor tomb I need, instead
Let them for me a bed
    Of twigs entwine.

That no one weeps my end,
    Nor for me grieves,
15 But let the autumn lend
    Tongues to the leaves,
When brooklet ripples fall
    With murmuring sound,
    And moon is found
20 Among the pine-trees tall,
    While softly rings
The wind its trembling chime
And over me the lime
    Its blossom flings.

<pre>
25   As I will then no more
           A wanderer be,
     Let them with fondness store
           My memory.
     And Lucifer the while,
30   Above the pine.
           Good comrade mine,
     Will on me gently smile;
           In mournful mood,
     The sea sing sad refrain . . .
35   And I be earth again
           In solitude.
</pre>

EPIGONES

When I recall the golden days Roumanian poesy has seen,
I sink as in a tide of dreams with ripples luminous, serene,
While all around me softly flows the long and tender flood of spring.
I see that boundless ocean night o'er which the stars spread out their
                                              sails,
5 Days with three suns upon their brows, and verdant groves with
                                            nightingales,
Clear springs that overflow with thought, and songs like rivers bubbling.

I see the poets who have built a language like a honeycomb:
Cichindeal, the golden mounthed, *Mumulean*, deep sorrow's home,
Prale, strange and twisted one and *Daniil*, the sad and small,
10 *Văcărescu*, sweetly singing love songs of the springs that pass,
Cantemir upon the cloth planning out in knives and glass,
And *Beldiman* bold trumpeting of enemies in battle fall.

Sihleanu, silver lyre, *Donici* who was reason's nest,
Who, as rarely comes to happen, meditating, oft is dressed
15 In ears that are as donkey's long, or horns, or some such other guise;
Where is his so sagacious ox, and where his fox with cunning wiles?
They all have passed along the road that reaches on for endless miles,
With *Pann* they're gone, Pepelea's child, as clever as a proverb wise.

Eliad built his songs from dreams and out of legends' ancient glow,
20 From reading much the holy books, far prophecies of bitter woe,

Truth bathed in myth, or like the sphinx imbued with wisdom's
                                                      sunset gleam,
Mountain strange, with face of stone, that stands amid the gale of time,
And still today before the world an undeciphered riddling rhyme,
Rears up its head of towering rock amidst the clouds' unending stream.

25 *Bolliac* sings of slavedom days, and slavery's heavy brazen bands;
And warrior nations flock to arms where dark *Cîrlova's* banner stands,
Before the present's eyes he makes forgotten ages to appear;
Like *Byron,* who did loud awake the savage wind of passion's pain,
Pale *Alexandrescu* who put out the sacred lamp of hope again
30 Deciphering age-long chaos in the ruin of a single year.

Upon a bed with snow-white shroud, aye, swanlike in her death,
Reclined the maid with lashes long, sweet voice, and gentle breath;
Her life was one continual spring, her dying but one soft regret,
And there her poet lover stood, bound in her fresh young beauty's spell
35 And from his lyre sweet music poured, and from his eyes the hot
                                                          tears fell;
From such a source *Bolintineanu* did tenderly his songs beget.

Mureşan shakes rusty chains when his voice is raised in ire
And with his hand benumbed and lame can snap a hawsers threefold
                                                              wire;
He calls the very stones to life, as did the ancient myth narrate,
40 Sings the mountains and their pain, the pine-trees and their destiny;
For all his poorness mighty rich, shines like a planet fearlessly,
The priest of our awakening, the prophet of the signs of fate.

Negruzzi wipes away the dust from parchment that the past records
Within whose mouldy pages lie the tales of far Roumanian lords
45 In curious letters traced of old by trembling hand of many a clerk;

Dipping his brush in the secret well of the hues of history's days gone past,
He takes those times' dull canvasses and touches them to life at last
Portraying perhaps some tyrant prince who ruled the land in ages dark.

And now that of all our poets, the ever young, the always gay,
50 Who *doina* sings upon the leaves, as from a flute he pours his lay,
Alecsandri the merry heart, who does his sparkling story tell
As though he might be threading pearls upon a star-beam as it goes;
A luminous and glowing stream of gems that through the ages flows,
And laughs maybe amid his tears while singing what *Dridri* befell.

55 Or dreaming of a shadow pale, with folded wings of silver white,
And eyes that like twin legends with glow a deep and mystic light,
A smile as pure as Mary's own, and a voice like the sound of bells,
He places on her starry brow a diadem with jewels sown;
To rule a rebel world of men, he sets her on a golden throne,
60 And from his overflowing love the *poet's vision* softly wells.

Or dreaming when the shepherd lad soft pipes sweet *doina's* plaintive
strain,
A dream of waters deep, of cliffs that rise sublime above the plain,
A dream of ancient forests dark which rest upon the mountains' brow,
He wakes again within our hearts the yearning for our father's land
65 Till history like an icon fair takes form beneath his skillful hand
And mighty Stephen, sombre lord, comes back again to live an'now.
....
And here are we, the epigones, of fickle feeling, broken lyre,
Devoid of days, but passions strong, with aged hearts and ugly, dire
And mocking mask, with which to hide a face both hard and lined
with hate.
70 Our God naught but a shadow show, our country's name an idle sound,
Who seek to hide our emptiness in works of varnish without ground:
You trusted in your art, but *we believe in neither self nor fate.*

And therefore sacred are your words and destined to eternity,
For in your minds were they conceived and by your flooded hearts
                                                                set free;
75 Great souls have you, and ever fresh you keep your youth though
                                                                you grow old
The world has turned its wheel about, *the future* lies within your hand;
We are the past; like sapless trees forlorn and desolate we stand;
And all our works are false and faint, and meaningless and cold.

Lost in your dreams you stood apart, conversing with ideals high;
80 We smear the sea with painted waves, we patch with tinsel stars the sky;
And this because our heaven is grey, the sea is frozen round our shores.
You follow with tumultuous flight the mounted glory of your thought
And in among the gleaming stars on sky-born wings you lightly sport,
While up the comets' blazing track your spirit in its swiftness soars

85 Pale wisdom, understanding's child, her sacred taper burning gold,
Her royal smile as of a star that never sets, that grows not old,
Unshades her light to guide your path, to make secure your flowery road.
Your soul is of the angels born, your heart a silver lute becomes,
Across whose strings a song is stirred, the mellow wind of poetry
                                                                strums;
90 And to your eyes the earth is built, an icon hanging kings' abode.

But we to whom no vision comes look out with barren sightless stare
We ape the feelings we have not, we see false pictures everywhere;
We call you poets mystic fools and fitting subjects for our mirth.
All is convention: truth today, tomorrow will become a lie.
95 Aye, you have fought your fight in vain, the present does the past deny;
You, who have dreamt of golden days upon this grey, this bitter earth.

Life has no other scope than death, and after death is life again,
No other reason has the world, no gap within the endless chain;

Men raise up worshipped images, build systems that they deem exact,
100 And call them beautiful or good, according to their varying lights,
Dividing into many kinds their fine philosophies and rites
And casting fancy's finery upon the naked flesh of fact.

Tell me what is holy thought? A luminous but misty look
Of formless nonexistings set in a sad and tangled book
105 Made to confuse the minds of men, if they should chance to read
therein.
And what is poetry? An angel pale with crystal gaze,
Voluptuous pictures, trembling sounds. With heavenly toys the poet
plays —
A robe of purple and of gold laid on a mortal creature's skin.

I bid farewell to all you poets dreaming fanciful fantastic dreams,
110 Who gave the rolling waves their music and the stars their silver
beams,
Who built upon this world of clay a greater world where thought
is free;
Today our heads are laid in *dust*, behold, tomorrow death is here
Genius, dullard, sound and soul, the common end of all is near,
The earth is naught but flying dust . . . and of this flying dust are we.

CĂLIN

(Pages from a tale)

Gazel   *Autumn come, the dead leaves flying,*
A cricket somewhere softly crying,
A sad breeze whispering at your window,
The pane with trembling fingers prying,
5 *While you're awaiting gentle sleep*
Alone before your fireplace lying.
What made you start and raise your head,
Was is a foot the stairway trying?
Aye, 'tis your lover come at last,
10 *Around your waist his strong arm plying.*
Before your face he holds a mirror,
Wherein your loveliness espying,
You gaze upon its image long
And linger, dreaming, smiling, sighing.

I

15 Over the hill the moon ascends her fiery crown of crimson deep,
Staining the ancient forest red, and the lonely castle keep,
And staining red the tumbling waves that from a murmuring fountain
                                                well,
While down the sweeping valley rolls the solemn music of a bell.
Above the river's rocky course rises the castle grim and tall
20 While, clinging fast against its face, a knight is scaling high the wall;
Clambering up on hands and knees, and holding tight to crack and edge,
Until the rusty bars he breaks that issue from a window ledge.

Silently he passes through, and soft, on tiptoe, does he creep
Into a secret chamber where the wall is hung with shadow deep
25 And where the starry sky between the bars and tangled creepers gleams
And timidly and unassured the broken moonlight softly streams;
Where strikes the moon the walls and floor are white as though they
had been chalked,
But darkness lies where shadows fall, as black as though with charcoal
marked.

Down from the ceiling to the floor has an enchanted spider spun
30 A wonder web, more light and fair than e'er by human weaver done.
It trembles in the silver light as though its veil would surely tear
Beneath the weight of misty gems that shine upon its filet there.
Beyond the web, in magic sleep, the sovereign's lovely daughter lies,
Drenched in the moon's unearthly light, before the knight's enraptured
eyes.
35 Beneath the sheet her form he sees, her sleeping body young and fair,
For the silken coverings hide it but little from his stare,
And here and there her sleeping gown parted a little leaves to show
The secret lovely nakedness of girlish limbs as white as snow.
Upon her pillow's smooth incline her heavy golden hair is laid,
40 While on her temples gently throb her pulses in a violet shade:
Arched eyebrows finely marked across the marble of her face,
Drawn as though in one straight line, in noble and bewitching grace.
Beneath the curtain of lids, her eyes in slumber seem to beat,
While one smooth rounded shapely arm lies nakedly upon the sheet.
45 Her full and gently moving breast in maiden ripeness tender shows
And through her lips, a bit apart, her burning breath in silence flows.
Her delicate and lovely mouth moves sweetly in a wistful smile,
While over her and round her head a mound of fragrant petals pile.

But now the knight draws near her bed and stretching out his
hand he tears
50 The spider's sparkling wonder web and spills the precious gems it bears.
Upon her beauty's nakedness he feeds his hungry heart's desire
And scarcely can his breast contain the burning ardor of its fire;

Till clasping her to him at last in one long, clinging sweet caress,
His scarlet mouth is set on hers, and on her lips his hot lips press.
55 Then taking from her hand a ring, glittering with jewels dear,
Turns, and through the moonlit casement goes our dauntless cavalier.

II

When morning comes, and the wondering maid finds that the web is
                                                    broken through
And in her mirror sees her lips by thirsty kisses bruised and blue,
Sadly she smiles and softly says, while gazing on her image white;
60 "O dauntless, dark curled fairy prince, come back again to me tonight".

III

Each one of us has private notions about sweet maidens and their ways,
But no man in his sense will doubt that they love best themselves to
                                                    praise.
Just as Narcissus saw his face framed in the water's silver glass
And finding he was fair, at once the lover and the loved one was.
65 If we could only see the maid when she essays her winning airs,
When all alone with wide round eyes she at her mirrored image stares,
See the provoking, pouting lips moving to call herself by name,
And she herself more lovable than all the world does soft acclaim;
He that is wise in maidens' ways would read her secret at a glace,
70 And know the lovely lass has grown aware of her own elegance.
Idol thou, o thief of wits, great blue eyes and golden hair,
. The worship of your maiden heart has chosen too an idol fair !
What does she whisper secretly, what words of love does she bestow
Upon the figure mirrored there, which she regards from top to toe?
75 "A beauteous dream I had indeed, a fairy prince who came by night.
I almost squeezed the life from him, my arm about him clasped so tight.
And thus it is, with outstretched arms, my gaze my image does carress
When I before my mirror stand alone in all my nakedness,
And like a cloak against my sides my heavy hanging golden hair,

129

80 When I regard myself and smile, and fain would kiss my shoulder bare,
   Until the blood mounts to my face for very shame of my desires,
   O fairy prince why don't you come to quench the flame my being fires?
   If in my body I rejoice, if I find pleasure in my eyes,
   It is because I see 'tis there the wonders of *his* passion rise;
85 The love I lavish on myself is only of his love a part.
   Mouth, learn wisdom's quick restraint, lest you betray my loving heart
   Even to him who steals by night to the couch on which his loved one lies,
   Be passionate as a woman is, but as an artful child be wise".

IV

   So every night the fairy prince does to her bedside softly creep
90 And with a sweet enchanted kiss awake her gently from her sleep.
   And when he to the window goes to flee before the dawn away,
   She will retain him with her eyes and humbly pleading she will say:
   "O stay, o go not with the dawn, think of the fiery vows you made,
   Do not depart, my black-locked prince, o luckless and ill-fated shade.
95 You will not find in wandering through all the endless ways of space
   A soul to love you as I do, you will not find a fairer face.
   Sweet is the shadow of your eyes with depth of sadness unsurpassed,
   May no one on your luckless course the evil eye upon you cast".
   Then to her bed he comes again, about her waist his strong arms steal,
100 She whispers words of tender love, whispers which her fiery kisses seal.
   He murmurs: "Whisper on, dear love, and let thy eyes' soft mystery
   Speak on in meaningless sweet words, that full of meaning are to me.
   Life's golden moment, swift as light, as transient as the rising smoke,
   I dream entire when with my hands thy mouth and shapely
                                              arm I stroke,
105 When on my breast you lean your head feeling my heart's enamoured
                                              beat
   And I in passion press my lips upon your rounded shoulder sweet;
   And when our thirsty lips unite, I drink thy breath into my soul,
   Our hearts grown heavy in our breasts, that each the other's pain console.
   When, lost in ecstasy of love, you hold your burning cheek to mine,
110 And when your long, soft golden hair about my neck you gently twine,

130

And when at last you close your eyes and generously your kisses give,
Then am I happiest of men, the height of joy superlative...
And you... but no, I have no words, my tongue is tied and cannot
move,
I would, and yet I cannot speak... I cannot tell you how I love".
115 Thus would they talk and so much say, such happiness was in them
springing,
Yet often was their discourse checked, their lips so often sweetly clinging,
Thus clasped in close embrace they lay, drinking of lover's joy their fill.
Till silent grew their lips at last, although their eyes were speaking still
And bashfully she covered up her face, with soft confusion red,
120 And hid her tearful eyes within her shining hair of golden thread.

V

Now white and waxen is your face that ruddy like an apple shone,
And your smooth and lovely cheeks have shrunken grown and thin
and wan.
Now from your eyes your silken tresses wipe many a sad despairing tear
That from your broken heart is sent. Disenchanted you appear,
125 Standing thus before your window, with no word upon your lips.
Now you raise your long wet lashes, and out of the room your sad
soul slips,
Soaring up the limpid heavens where the tireless lark does fly.
You would call for him to take you with him up the shining sky.
The bird flies on quite unawares while you with tearful eyes remain,
130 Your luckless lips devoid of speech, trembling as though in pain.
O do not quench in useless weeping the light that gleams from your
blue eyes;
Do not forget that in their tears the secret of their beauty lies.
Thus, silver drops, from heaven's space, the falling stars descend like rain,
But ere they cross the deep blue vault they are each one recaught again,
135 For should they weep their tears away the heavens would be blind and
bare.
Fruitless is it that you essay to span the lofty dome of air.
The night of moonshine and of stars, of streams like mirrors shining
bright

131

Cannot be likened anyway unto the tomb's dark endless night.
It does but lend your beauty charm if now and then a tear be shed,
140 But if you drain the fountains dry, how shall they be replenished?
Let the colour gain your cheeks, as proud   and lovely as a rose,
Your youthful cheeks that now are pale as violet shaded mountain
snows.
Your eyes give back their violet night that all eternity endears,
But which so swiftly is destroyed beneath the track of bitter tears.
145 Who is there who is mad enough to burn on coals an emerald rare,
That all its lovely lustrous shine be lost and squandered in the air?
You veil your eyes' dark brilliancy to waste your beauty unbeguiled,
And knows the world not what it lacks. O weep no more, you hapless
child.

VI

O king, with long and tangled beard, like twisted hanks of cotton wool,
150 There is no wisdom in your brains: with bran and dust your skull is full.
Are you well pleased to be alone, you sorry joker, weak and old,
Sighing o'er your daughter's lot, your pipe between your teeth grown
cold,
As now you pace the corridor, numbering again its bare white boards?
Poor are you now in very truth, that once had riches beyond words.
155 Your daughter you have driven out, to some far corner of the earth,
That in a mean and lonely hut to a young prince she should give birth.
In vain you send your messengers to search for her the whole world
round,
For not a single one of them can guess the place she may be found.

VII

Grey are the autumn evenings now; the water of the lake is grey,
160 A thousand ripples cross its face to hide among the reeds away;
While through the forest gently sighs a wind that takes the withered
leaves
And shakes them softly to the ground, a passing wind that sadly heaves

132

The boughs. Till now the forest branches stripped of all their leaves
are bare
And does the lonely moon unchecked her beams of silver squander
there.
165 In melancholy harmonies the brook is murmuring its distress
The wailing breeze snaps off a twig and nature dons her saddest dress.
But who is this that wanders down the steep and winding forest
track,
This youth who o'er the valley throws his eagle eyes of fiery black?
O dark-haired prince, seven years have passed since when you climbed
the castle wall,
170 Have you forgot the lovely maid that loved you well and gave you all?
Now in the open field he sees a little, bright, barefooted child
Endeavouring to drive along a quacking brood of ducklings wild.
"Good day to you, my lad", he cries . . . "Good day brave stranger,"
says the lad.
"Tell me what's your name young man". "Călin, the name my father
had.
175 Whenever I my mother ask whose boy I am she says the same:
A fairy prince your father is, and Călin also is his name".
And as he listens only he knows how his heart leaps up with joy
To see this child that drives the ducks and recognize him as his boy
He enters now the narrow hut where, at a wooden bench's end,
180 A rushlight in an earthen pot its feeble yellow light does spend.
Two large round cakes he finds are set to bake upon the hearth's rude
stone;
One shoe is flung beneath a beam and one behind the door is thrown.
An old and dented coffee-mill somewhere in a corner lies,
While near the fire a sleek tomcat purrs and cleans its ears and eyes
185 Beneath the icon of a saint, hanging besmoked upon the wall,
A little *candela* is hung, as poppy seed its flame is small.
Below the icon on a shelf are thyme and mint arranged in heaps,
From which throughout the darkened hut a hot and peppery fragrance
seeps.
Upon the dingy plaster walls and on the stone besmeared with clay
190 The infant, with a charcoal stick, has drawn, to wile the time away,

133

Pigs with corkscrew curling tails and little trotters drawn like twigs,
The kind that really most become all self-respecting piggie-wigs.
Acroos the tiny window frame a bladder stretched in place of glass,
Through which but faint and gloomy rays into the cottage dimly pass.
195 Upon a bed of simple boards, motionless the princess lies,
Her face towards the window turned, but closed in sleep her lovely
eyes.

He sits beside her on the bed, he lays his hand upon her brow,
And sadly he caresses her, he sighs and fondles her, and now,
Bending down his lips to her, quietly her name he calls,
200 Till, opening her drowsy eyes o'er which a fringe of lashes falls,
Terrified she starts and stares, believing it is all a dream;
Fain would she smile but does not dare, she is afraid yet dares not
scream.
He lifts her from her narrow bed and holds his arms around her fast,
His heart so beats within his breast he feels that it must burst at last.
205 She stares at him and still she stares, but not a single world is said,
Then laughs with brimming tearful eyes, before this miracle afraid.
Around her finger long and white she twists a mesh of raven hair,
Then falls upon his ready breast to hide from him her blushes there.
He smoothes away the kerchief that wraps and covers up her head,
210 And tenderly with burning lips does kiss that crown of golden thread.
She raises up her face to his, her eyes, in which sparkling tears spring
And fondly do their lips unite, and each does to the other cling.

VIII

If through the copper woods you pass, the silver woods shine far away,
There you will hear a thousand throats proclaim the forest's roundelay.
215 The grass beside the bubbling spring shines like snow in sunlight fair
And blue flowers drenched in moisture rise and tremble in the perfumed
air.
It seems the tall and ancient trees have souls beneath their barks
concealed,
Souls that oft amid their boughs by singing voices are revealed,
While down the hidden forest glades, beneath the twilight's silver haze,

220 One sees the rapid brooklets leap along their shining pebbly ways.
In hurrying, gleaming ripples bright, sighing among the flowers they go
And tumbling down the torrent's track murmur and gurgle as they flow,
Swelling in liquid masses clear over the shallow gravel beds,
A swirling, eddying, dancing stream, on which the moon her silver sheds.
225 Many small blue butterflies; and many a swarm of golden bees
Busy at visiting the honey flowers pass in among the trees,
And a host of darting, shining flies of different kinds and hues
Make the summer air vibrate with colours that the eyes confuse.

Beside the sleepy trembling lake, its waters softly glimmering,
230 Stands a *long table* over which the torches' flames are shimmering.
Emperors and empresses from North and South and West and East
Are come to meet the lovely bride and celebrate that weddings feast,
Paladins with golden hair and dragons dressed in wondrous mail,
Magicians and astrologers, and the clown Pepele gay and pale.
235 Above them all the aged king sits in his royal high-backed chair,
Upon his head he wears a crown, has trimmed his beard and combed
his hair.
Bolt upright on cushions high he sits, his sceptre in his hand
And is, lest flies should trouble him, by willow bearing pages fanned.
Now out of the forest's black retreat advances Călin, by his side,
240 Her hand within her bridegroom's hand, his radiant and smiling bride.
As they come near one hears the leaves rustle beneath her rich long
dress.
She has her cheeks flushing with pleasure and her eyes sparkling with
joy.
Sweeping almost to the ground billows her soft and golden hair,
Falling about her shapely arms and over her white shoulders bare.
245 Gracefully indeed she moves, carries herself with noble mien,
Upon her brow she wears a star and in her hair blue flowers are seen.
The king bids all the guests to seat themselves, the feast is then
begun.
For bridesmaid does he name the moon, for groomsman names the sun.
The guests about the table sit according to their rank and years,
250 The *cobza* and the violin play softly to delighted ears.
But what strange music sounds beside? Low as a swarm of bees
it hums.

135

The guests in wonder stare around, but none can tell from whence
it comes.

Till they descry a cobweb vast hung like a bridge across the glade
O'er which a multitude of beasts rush by in murmuring cascade.

255 Ants in hundreds carrying sacks of flour and little lumps of yeast
In their strong mouths, to bake puddings and cakes for the wedding
feast,

Bees with honey from the comb and pure gold dust upon their thighs,
From which the woodworm, goldsmith fine, will make fantastic
jewelries.,

Till lastly comes the wedding train, a cricket bears the usher's rod,
260 While round him leaps a host of fleas, their tiny feet in iron shod.
In a portentous velvet robe straddles a great potbellied drone,
Who in a drowsy nasal drawl mimicks the priestly monotone.
Grasshoppers pull a nutshell coach, the cobweb shakes as it goes by
Within it, curling his moustache, reclines the bridegroom butterfly.

265 And after him there comes a host of butterflies of every sort
In lighthearted cavalcade, playful, gallant, full of sport.
Mosquitoes form the orchestra, here are beetles, there are snails.
The bride, a timid violet moth, shelters behind her trailing veils.
Upon the table spread, the nimble usher cricket takes a spring,

270 Rises upon his hind legs, bows, and clicks his spurs so that they ring;
Then coughs and buttons up his coat and says, ere the amazement ceased,
"Pardon us, Lords and Ladies, if we have by yours our wedding feast"

GHOSTS

. . . for it fades away like smoke above the earth·
They bloomed like flowers, were cut like grass,
Wrapped up in a linen and buried in the ground

I

Within an ancient church with lofty soaring dome,
Between tall waxen candles, does in her coffin lie,
Her face towards the altar, wrapped in white drapery,
The bride ot brave King Harold, the King of Avari,
5 While softly chanted dirges do from the darkness come.

Upon the dead girl's breast a wreath of jewels glows,
Her golden hair hangs loosely over the coffin side,
Her eyes are sunken deep; a sad smile sanctified
Rests on her parched lips, that death to mauve has dyed,
10 While is her lovely face as pale as winter snows.

Beside her on his knees is Harold, mighty King,
And from his bloodshot eyes does shine untold despair,
His mouth with pain is drawn, dishevelled is his hair.
Though like a lion he would roar, grief holds him silent there;
15 Three days he thinks upon his life in nameless sorrowing.

"I was still but a child. Within the pine-tree glade
My greedy eyes already had conquered many a land;
I dreamed an empire grow beneath my fancy's wand,
I dreamed the world entire was under my command,
20 The foaming Volga's ford I fathomed with my blade.

137

Countless mighty hosts my youthful zeal led forth
By whom as of some God my name was worshipped.
I felt the very earth tremble beneath my tread;
Before my marching hosts the wandering nations fled,
25   Crowding in their terror the empty frozen North.

For Odin had deserted his frosty ancient home,
Down long and turtuous ways his wandering people went;
Priests with snowy locks and backs that time had bent
Roused and led through forests where peace an age had spent
30   Thousand diverse tongues along the way to Rome.

One eve my troops I camped upon the Dniestr's side,
Intending on the morrow your battle host to quell;
But there amidst your councillors I came beneath your spell;
Before your marble loveliness my eyes in wonder fell,
35   So fearless you stood, in all your childish pride.

Before your soft reproach my words dried on my tongue...
I strove to make an answer, but could no answer find.
Would earth have swallowed me, and left no trace behind,
My hands before my face I put my shame to blind,
40   And tears came to the eyes where tears had never sprung.

Your councillors did smile and soon departed then
To leave us quite alone. I asked you, after a space,
Though scarcely did I dare to look upon your face;
Why have you come, o Queen, into this desert place?
45   What do you seek so far away from courts and men?

In a murmur filled with tears, gentle and sad you spake
Holding me with your eyes in which the sky shone clear,

You said: « I beg of you, o King and cavalier,
To give to me as prisoner the one I hold most dear,
50   Harold, that untamed youth, him would I captive take. »

Turning my head away, I handed you my sword.
My people ceased their march along the Danube side;
Harold no longer dreamed the universe to ride,
His ears for tender tones and poetry did abide,
55   The conqueror from that hour was vanquished by your word.

From then sweet maid with hair of gold as ripened grain
Each night you came to me when nobody should know,
And your white, slender arms around my neck did throw,
And raising coaxing lips to mine you said in whispers low:
60   « O, King, it is for Harold I come to beg again. »

If you would ask for Rome, if you would ask the earth,
Or all the corwns that rest on mortal monarch's head,
The wandering stars that beam across the heavens shed,
There heaped about your feet would I bestow instead,
65   But do not ask for Harold for he is nothing worth.

Ah, where are gone the days when brave I probed the ford
To stride into the world. Far better had it been
If so much loveliness my eyes had never seen ...
To ride through ruined towns, to lead the battle keen
70   And thus fulfil those dreams the pine-tree forest stored !''

The torches are raised up. The train moves slowly on.
The Danube Queen is carried down to her narrow bed,
Councillor and monarch with heavy drooping head,
Priests with snowy beards and eyes that tears shed,
75   Mumbling their dirge in mounrful unison.

Beneath the arching vault the slow procession goes,
A mystery religion, a strange and sombre lore,
They lower down the coffin beneath the gaping floor,
Then close it with a cross, a seal for evermore,
80 Beneath the holy lamp that in the corner glows.

Be silent, in God's name,
To hear the bay
Of the earth-hound
Under the stone cross.

II

Harold on his charger sweeps far o'er hill and dale,
Like a dream he goes within the moon's pale zone;
Across his breast in folds his black cloak he has thrown,
Behind him drifts of leaves high in the air are blown,
85 While never straight before him the Polar Star does sail.

Reaching at last the forest that clothes the rising hills,
Where does a sweet spring murmur, well out from 'neath a stone,
Where grey with scattered ashes an old hearth stands alone,
Where far off in the forest the earth-hound sounds his tone
90 And with his distant barking he midnight silence fills.

Upon a rocky ledge, quite stiff and ashen faced,
There sits, with crutch in hand, a priest of pagan creed
For ages sits he thus, by death forgot indeed,
Moss growing on his forehead and on his breat long weed,
95 His beard reaching to the ground, his eyebrows to his waist.

Blindly thus for ages he sits both day and night,
Until his feet have grown one with the stone at last,
Numbering the days that numberless have passed,
While over him are circling in endless circles vast
100 Two crows on weary wings, one black, the other white.

140

And now upon his arm the youth doth sudden lay
His eager hand, and wakes the old priest terrified:
"To you, o timeless Seer, across the world I ride
To give me back the one that envious death does hide,
105   And all my days for you I will unceasing pray."

Now with his crutch the Seer his heavy eyebrows parts
And gazes on the King, but not an utterance makes.
Then out o'the stone's grey substance his feet with trouble takes
And turning towards the forest his battered crutch he shakes,
110   And lastly up the narrow path with heavy paces starts.

Upon the oaken doorway that guards the mountain keep
With crutch on high uplifted loud three times does he knock;
With thunderous commotion the gates slow backwards rock,
The priest kneels down . . . while through the young king's spirit flock
115   A thousand dreadful fears, and thousand terrors leap.

Into the lofty vault of shining marble black
They go. The door swings shut again with rumbling sound;
The Seer now lights a candle that spreads its glow around
And throws away behind them their shadows on the ground
120   And lights the sombre walls that shine like iron back.

There in the dreadful darkness they know not what will come . . .
The old magician makes a sign that he should bide,
And Harold crouches down, his sword clasped at his side,
While nameless, awful dread does through his spirit ride,
125   Blank gazing at the walls of that uncanny tomb.

Till soon the Seer did seem immeasurably to grow;
He waved his magic crutch above his ancient head,

141

And through the chilly vault a wind in wailing sped
And thousand whispering voices into the silence shed
130   A song the filled the dome with gentle cadence low.

And now the singing gradually increases like a breeze
Until with sudden swelling it to a tempest grows,
As though a gale that madly across the ocean blows,
As though the tortured soul of deepest earth arose
135   And all that lives and feels with horrid fright must freeze

The mighty vault now trembles from ceiling to the floor,
The marble walls are rocking and crack right to their base
While through the darkness curses do sobs in panic chase,
And cries and moans and lightning amidst the tumult race
140   Till thunderous indeed has grown the wild uproar ...

"Out of the heart of earth let man the dead awake,
And let the stars her eyes their pristine spark ignite,
Her golden hair the moon, like it was once, make bright,
While you, o Zalmoxis, eternal seed of light,
145   With breath of fire and frost let her of life partake.

Search wide throughout the kingdom where Harols is the King,
Search deep the very entrails of this revolving earth,
Out of ice make vapour, from stone make gold of worth,
Blood make out of water, and fire from rock give birth,
150   While in her maiden heart again let hot blood spring."

At that the walls enclosing withdraw before his eyes,
He sees the snow and lightning and ice as one conspire,
The sky, the wind, the water, the elements entire,

142

He sees a mighty city beneath a bridge of fire,
155 And over all a thunderstorm of wailing and of sighs.

He sees the Christian church bow'neath the tempest's host,
He sees the falling lightning its bulwarks shatter through,
The secret tomb within wide open laid to view,
The covering stone of marble divided now in two
160 And out of that uncoverd grave does rise ... a ghost.

A thing of snow she is. Upon her bosom frail
A wreath of rubies glows, her hair to earth arrayed,
Her eyes sunk in her head, her lips of violet shade,
Her hands as though of wax upon her temples laid,
165 Her tender childish face as new slaked lime is pale.

The tumult of her coming does all the clouds dispel,
The lightning and the thunder out of the heavens fly,
The moon turns pitchy-black within a drooping sky,
The waters sink to nowhere and leave the oceans dry;
170 An angel in her sleep, it seems, who walks through hell.

The vision fades away. Before those gleaming walls,
A form does now approach, with smooth and silent stride;
'Tis *she*. Harols stares, amazed with joy, wide eyed,
Then reaches out his arms to clasp her to his side,
175 But in a sudden trance to earth unconscious falls.

He feels two icy hands clasp gently round his heart,
A long and freezing kiss is set upon his breast,
As though from him in sleeping his very life would wrest ...
Then feels the life returning to her against him pressed
180 And knows that from that hour they nevermore will part.

'Tis verily the maid who in her coffin lay?
He feels in her the life yet ever warmer glow,
Till she around his neck her snowy arms does throw,
And raising coaxing lips she says in murmurs low:
185   "O King, behold Maria for Harold comes to pray!

Come, Harold, your sweet brow against my bosom lean;
Thou god with eyes of darkness ... how wonderful they shine!
But let me round your neck my golden hair entwine ...
My life and youth your presence does in the sky enshrine.
190   O let me gaze into your eyes of sweet and fatal sheen."

And now a sound of voices does gradually awake,
A song that ancient sweetness upon the ear bestows,
As when a spring at autumn among the dead leaves flows,
A harmony of love, voluptuous repose,
195   As when in silver cadence the breeze enfolds the lake.

*"... as often when people die, many of those
dead, they say, wake up to become ghosts ..."*

III

In high and empty halls the torches redly burn
Wounding like glowing coals the darkness they intrude;
Harold is striding there in madman's frenzied mood,
Harold, the youthful King; a King in solitude,
200   While all his palace seems to wait the dead's return.

Upon the marble mirrors a heavy shadow rears
Through which the torches' glimmer shines as on silken net,
A twilight doubly mournful with sorrowing beset;
The empty palace chambers house naught but dark regret,
205   While out of every corner it seems a dead man peers.

144

Since when the dome was shattered by dreadful lightning stroke
The whole day long he passes in cold and leaden sleep,
Upon his heart was branded a symbol black and deep.
But in the night he rises and does his council keep,
210 And then the pallid king does don his gloomy cloak.

It seems that now a mask of wax King Harold wears,
So paled and so still the face his griefs conceal;
Yet burn his eyes like fires, his lips the blood reveal,
Upon his heart he carries a black and deadly seal,
215 While on his noble forehead an iron crown he bears.

Since then in death's dark garments he wraps his life forlorn,
He cares but for sad chants as does the tempest play;
Often'neath the moon at midnight rides away,
And when he does return his eyes are bright and gay
220 Until death's shuddering voice will grasp him at the dawn.

Harold, what can mean this sombre funeral guise,
This face your wear like wax, so pale and motionless?
What is this seal, this scar that does your heart oppress,
Why do you light the funeral torch, love dirges of distress?
225 Harold, you are dead if I believe my eyes!

Today once more he mounts his fiery Arab horse
And o'er the wilderness he speeds with arrow's flight
While does the moon shine down her soft and silver light.
Now over the horizon Maria comes in sight,
230 And through the whispering forest the wind flies on its course.

Set in her golden hair a wreath of rubies gleams,
The light of many saints does in her large eyes sleep.

On towards the meeting place their chargers swiftly sweep.
They meet and each in greeting bows to the other deep
235 *But on their scarlet lips are stains of blood it seems.*

They gallop like the tempest with thousand wings, they fly
Speeding o er the country their chargers side by side,
Speaking of their love that naught can more divide,
She rests upon his arm that is around her plied
240 And on his ready shoulder her golden head does lie.

"Come Harold, your sweet brow upon my bosom lean,
Thou God with eyes of darkness... how beautiful they shine!
But let me round your neck my golden hair entwine...
My life and youth your presence does in the sky enshrine.
245 O let me gaze into your eyes of sweet and fatal sheen."

A soft and soothing scent is in the air dispersed,
A shower of lime-tree blossoms the wind in passing throws
Upon the way by which the Queen of Danube goes,
A murmuring of breezes among the petals blows,
250 While do in tender kiss unite their lips athirst.

Thus flying like the wind they each of love inquire,
Nor see beyond the night the dawn already glowing;
Yet in their souls they feel an icy shiver growing
And o'er their pallid faces a mask of death is showing
255 While slowly on their lips their whispered words expire.

"O Harold, on your breast allow my face to hide,
Do you not hear far off the cock's hoarse morning cry?
A spear of light that sprang athwart the eastern sky
To wound his fleeting life within my heart does pry;
260 Within my soul is born the ruddy fire of day."

146

Harold bolt upright was stricken like an oak,
His eyes forever veiled with death's eternal shade.
Their steeds fled on untended with panic dread afraid,
Like to a demon's shadow straight out of Hades strayed
265 They went ... Among the trees a plaintive wind awoke.

They speed on like a whirlwind, cross rivers no bridge spanned.
Before their flying course the dawn-lit mountains gleam,
They traverse hill and valley, and many a fordless stream,
Upon their waxen foreheads their crowns like lightning beam,
270 While far away before them the pine-tree forests stand.

Now from his rocky throne the old magician spies
Their coming, and he calls above the tempest fray
The sun to check its course, the night its moon delay,
The gale to fly abroad, the earth its movement stay,
275 Too late ... The rising sun is mounting up the skies.

The hurricane let loose a tale of pain relates
And sweeps along besides them to fill their steeds with dread;
Their eyes are dimmed and downcast, the fire in them is shed,
Beautiful their dying, in death forever wed.
280 Now, widely swinging, open the temple's double gates.

They ride into the temple, the gates behind them swing.
Lost for all eternity within the tomb's constraint;
Around them in the darkness there sounds a sad complaint,
For that fair mortal maid whose face was of a saint,
285 For Harold, youthful monarch, the pine-tree forest's king.

The Seer now lowers his eyebrows, the world fades from his sight,
His feet into the granite again enrooted grow,

Numbering the days that numberless did flow,
Harold in his failing mind a tale of long ago,
290   While soaring o'er his head two crows: one black, one white.

Upon his rocky ledge, upright and ashen faced,
There sits with crutch in hand the priest of pagan creed.
For ages sits he thus, by death forgot indeed,
Moss growing on his forehead and on his breast long weed,
295   His beard reaching to the ground, his eyebrows to his waist.

SATIRE I

When my eyes are weighed with sleep I quench the evening candle's
glow
And leave the ticking clock alone along the path of time to go;
When from my square of window-pane I draw the curtain to one side
The climbing moon pours in and floods the room with her voluptuous
light;
5 Then from the night of memory in answer to her summons steal
An endless host of sorrows pale that we have lived but now scarce feel.

Moon, fair ruler of the sea, over the sky's round vault you glide,
The sight of you recalls the griefs that locked within man's bosom bide;
Beneath thy virgin glow are there a thousand deserts glittering,
10 And thousand forest shades conceal the wells from which their waters
spring !
Over how many million waves extends thy timeless empery
When on your way you sail above the lonely wonder of the sea !
How many flower besprinkled fields, how many a walled and peopled
place
Have known your proud despotic charm when they but looked upon
your face !
15 Into how many thousand rooms you peered as now in mine you peer,
How many thousand brows has lit the flooded glory of thy sphere !
I see a king sit down to plot earth's destiny for endless days
While here the trembling beggar-man plans for the morrow scarcely
lays . . .

Different the lots these twain have drawn out of the secret urn of fate
20 Alike they fall beneath thy sway, alike inherit death's estate;
Whate'er they be they come alike under human passions' rule,
So as the weak man is the strong, so as the genius is the fool.
One searches on the mirror's face a novel way to curl his hair,
Another roves through time and space to track truth to her hidden lair,
25 Piling endless loads of lore from ancient learnings' yellow page
And noting down the thoughts and names that sped across some
bygone age.
Another from his counting house controls a nation's destinies
And figures gold his ships have brought across a score of troubled seas.
And here the old philosopher, his coat is torn, his elbows thin;
30 He works his brains without a pause, and does a web of logic spin.
Shivering with cold he buttons up his torn and ragged gown,
Turns up the collar round his neck, presses his cotton ear-plugs down;
Dried up and twisted as he is, of no importance does he stand
And yet he holds the universe within the ambit of his hand;
35 Within the confine of his brain the future and the past unite
And with his science he lays bare the secrets of eternal night.
As Atlas was of old declared to bear the sky upon his back,
So does our old philosopher the world within a cyphetack.
The moon looks in and sheds its beams a pile of ancient books upon,
40 He sets his mind to roving back across a thousand ages gone
Into the time are things began, when being and not being still
Did not exist to plague man's mind, and there was neither life nor will,
When there was nothing that was hid, yet all things darkly hidden were,
When self-contained was uncontained and all was slumber everywhere.
45 Was there a heavenly abyss? Or yet unfathomable sea?
There was no mind to contemplate an uncreated mystery.
Then was the darkness all so black sa seas that roll deep in the earth,
As black as blinded mortal eye, and no man yet had come to birth,
The shadow of the still unmade did not its silver threads unfold,
50 And over an unending peace unbroken empty silence rolled!...
Then something small in chaos stirred ... the very first and primal
cause.
And God the Father married space and placed upon confusion laws.

That moving something, small and light, less than a bubble of sea spray,
Established through the universe eternal and unquestioned sway...
55 And from that hour the timeless mists draw back their dark and
hanging folds
And law in earth and sun and moon essential form and order moulds.
After that day in endless swarms countless flying worlds have come
Out of the soundless depth of space, each drawn towards its unknown
home,
Have come in shining colonies rising from out infinity,
60 Attracted to the universe by strange and restless urge to be,
While we, inheritors of space, the children of this world of awe,
Are raising witless heaps of sand upon our little earthy floor;
Microscopic nations rise with warrior and king and seer,
Throughout the years our fortunes wax, until we have forgotten fear.
65 We, flies, that for a single day buzz in a measured world and small,
Suspended in the midst of time, careless and forgetting all
That this frail world in which we trust is only flung momentarily
Between the darkness that is past and all the darkness yet to be.
Just as the motes of dust enjoy their kingdom in the lamplight's ray,
70 Thousand specks that are no more when once that beam has passed
away
So, in the midst of endless night, we have our little time to spend,
Our moment snatched from chaos, which did not yet come to an end.
But when our beam at last goes out, our world will suddenly disperse
Amidst the dark that ever hangs around this whirling universe.

75 Yet not within the present day stays the philosopher's quick thought;
One cast of that far-ranging brain a hundred eons of time has caught.
He sees grow small and red and cold the sun that now burns high
and proud,
And at last he sees it die closing like a wound stabbed in a cloud.
He sees the rebel planets freeze and headlong plunge about in space
80 Freed from the ordering of the sun who deep in night has veiled his face.
While o'er earth's altar like a veil eternity its darkness weaves
And one by one pale, faded stars are falling like the autumn leaves.

The body of the universe is stiffened to eternal death
And through the emptiness of space is neither movement, life nor
breath.
85 All falls into not being's night and an unbroken silence reigns
As once again the universe its primal peace and void regains . . .

. . . .

Commencing with the multitude that swarms uncounted on the ground
And rising to the palace where the Emperor sits with glory crowned,
All are as one, and each is by the riddle of *his* life pursued,
90 And none can say which man of them is most with misery endued,
For unto *all* comes *each* man's lot, to *all* the fate of *each* applies.
Little it aids if one of them above his class succeeds to rise
While all the others stay below and gaze on him with humble hearts,
For he and they are all unknown, playing the same ephemeral parts.
95 What reckons fate of their desires, what *they* would have, or do, or be?
Fate rides as blindly o'er their lives as does the wind across the sea.

Now writers out of every land and all the world high plaudits raise . . .
What cares the old philosopher? And what to him is all men's praise?
Immortality, people will say! True, all his hard lived days were spent
100 In clinging to a single thought, as ivy round a tree is bent.
"After I die," he tells himself, "my name will live to endless time,
From age to age, from mouth to mouth, and carried to the farthest
clime,
Unto the farthest realms of earth, and to the world's remotest mind'
Behind the rampart of my works may not my name a refuge find?'
105 Poor soul! Do you yourself retain everything that passed your head?
All the dreams that you have dreamed, all the words that you have said?
Little enough: but here and there some thread of images, some bit
Of tattered thought, some phrase, some scrap of yellow paper closely
writ.
If you forget the life you had, the things that you have done and seen,
110 Will other men spend fruitless days discovering how it must have been?
Perhaps somewhere in days to come, some green-eyed pedant's gaze
will fall

Upon a pile of faded books, himself more faded than them all,
To scan the wonder of your words and weigh them in his niggard
scale,
While from their bindings dust will rise and on his glasses spread a veil.
115 Then will he place your works in rows upon his shelves and summaries
Upon a ragged paper slip; he'll write of your philosophies.

Though you create or sink a world, one end there is to all your toil,
For over you and all your works a spade will heap a mound of soil.
An emperor's head, or one in which a world of wisdom has been stored
120 Finds ample room within a box composed of four short bits
of board . . .
And all will hasten to attend the honoured funeral you will get,
Splendid in their irony, with posturings of feigned regret . . .
And from some carven pulpit tall a nobody will glibly prate;
Not for your honour will he speak, but on his own great gifts dilate
125 Under the shadow of your name: a windy, pompous, empty speech.

Posterity? What is it but a phantom far beyond your reach!
For who should dream posterity will ever think to talk of you,
Except perhaps in some small tome written with grudging words and
few,
Compiled by some old soulless scribe to prove that you were common
clay,
130 A man like any one of them. For fully satisfied are they
To prove you even as themselves. Their learned nostrils wide extending
Dilated with a splendid pride, when at some learned meeting's ending
Your name pedantically is used, knowing beforehand there will be,
Uttered by ironic mouth, some gilded word in praise of thee.
135 Fallen among these wolfish fools your glory will be torn to shreds,
While all that is not understood will be decried by wagging heads.
Then they will probe your private life, dissecting that, discounting this,
And searching out with eager eyes each little thing you've done amiss,
To make you even as themselves. They will not care for all the light

140 Your labour poured upon the world, but for the sins and every sligt
And human failing they can find, and every petty thing that must
Befall the life of hapless days, of every mortal child of dust.
And every little misery that harassed a tormented mind
Will seem more notable to them than all the truths that you did find.

• • • • • ˑ• ˑ• •

145 Within a garden's closing walls, where fruit-tree blossom strews the
ground,
And over which the full moon sails with all her shining splendour
crowned,
Out of the depth of memory's night countless hidden longings rise;
Pain is benumbed as in sleep, we see the world with dreamer's eyes,
For in the calm light of the moon fancy's gates are opened wide
150 And all around us phantoms creep after the candle light has died . . .
Beneath thy virgin glow, o moon, are thousand deserts glittering,
And thousand forest shades conceal the wells from which their waters
spring !
Over how many million waves extends thy timeless empery
When on your way you sail above the lonely wonder of the sea !
155 All who sojourn on this earth, within the iron realm of fate,
Alike are subject to thy sway, alike inherit death's estate !

SATIRE II

Why does my rhyme-creating pen stand rusting in the ink you ask?
And why has poetry lost its power to tempt me from the daily task?
Why do I sleep my days away, with crushed in yellow pages there
Climbing iambus, trochees swift, and dactyl with the sprightly air?
5 If you but knew the worries all which fill my waking hours with care,
You'd see I have a wealth of words, enough to choke me and to spare.
But why, I ask, should I begin to shape again the song that's sung
And mould into a form that's new the metal of this wise old tongue?
To twist the secret ecstasies that lie asleep within my breast
10 To carefully painted couplets which are goods for sale among the
rest?
When hungrily I seek the form that best becomes their inward grace,
Why write to suit the world at large a legend on the water's face?

But you will say it would be well that all the corners of the earth
Should come to hear my lovely rhymes, and my name advertise its
worth
15 By tickling the illustrious ears of mighty men of high estate,
Or sweetly flattering verse, perhaps, to lovely ladies dedicate,
And so console my soul's disgust through the prostration of my mind.
Dear friend, the path you indicate is one by many trod I find.
The world can boast today a wealth of that most curious sort of bard
20 Who his poetry uses as a means to cultivate the great's regard;
By writing dexterous poems which the prowess of his patrons boom,
His songs in coffee-shops are heard, and in my lady's drawing-room.

Knowing the ways of life and how its narrow road the heart can vex,
Such poets launch their labours 'neath the shelter of the weaker sex,
25 And dedicate their little books to those whose husbands may by chance
As an appropriate reward their way in politics advance.
Why is it that I do not strive for glory's crown and honours grand?
What fame is there in standing up and preaching to the desert sand?
Today when to his sensual self each mortal man is bounden slave,
30 Renown is but the idle flag which many thousand dunces wave,
Who, raising up their Idol Gods, a dwarf like to a giant dress,
As bubbles floating in the air amidst an age of nothingness.

Or shall my lyre resound in praise of love? That chain held evenly
Between the hands of lovers two, sometimes the chain that bindeth
three.
35 What! Suttter on a silver chord where swelling harmony unfolds
And join the operetta where 'tis Menelaus the baton holds?
Women today, like all the world, are often but a kind of school,
Where we can study what is pain, and fraud and make-believe hold
rule;
To learn in these academies the votaries of Venus go,
40 Fond pupils who, the more they learn, the younger and more blatant
grow,
Till at the finish of the course we see them in the infant class,
And finally the precious school does into nameless ruin pass.

O, do you still recall the years through which we sweetly dreaming lay
And heard our learned teacher's mumble tailoring time's coat away?
45 The corpses of the moments gone he reassembled in the past
And searched around for wisdom in the odds and ends that time has
cast.
With bland and sleepy murmurings, an endless spring of *horum-harum*,
Babbling, blinking, pointing out *nervum reurm gerendarum*;
The mind's still windlass turning round in heavy, holy pondering,
50 And now some planet came to view, and now some great Egyptian king.

156

Meseems I see th'astronomer, yawning away in vaporous rest,
Take out the world from primal night as though wide chaos were a
chest,
And spread all time out like a rug; meseems I hear him thoughtfully
teach
How eons counted off like beads are threaded on a cotton each,
55 Talking, talking till the world awhirling in our heads we found,
And we like Galileo cried "Upon: my soul, it all goes round."
Till dazed by languages forgotten, planets, dates, scholastic rot.
We mixed our master with a king in who's beard the moths had got,
And gazing at the cobwebs thick that hung from roof and pillar too
60 We listened to king Ramses, and we dreamed . . . we dreamed sweet
eyes of blue.
While in the margin of our books we scribbed verses debonair,
It may be to a rose in bloom, or to Clotilda wild and fair;
While round us floated images caught up and tangled in time's net
Now of the sun, now of a king, and now of some domestic pet.
65 The scratching of our pens gave charm ot this array of bending backs
That like the sleepy ocean swelled, or rippled like a field of flax.
And soon oblivion covered all as bent arms pillowed heavy head
Until the clanging class-room bell proclaimed that Ramses must be dead.

Then, the realm of our fancy turned into reality,
70 While the actual world seemed a mere impossibility.
Now, we can see that for a heart loving truth and honesty
The only means becoming are so hard and wiry;
Dreaming is a real danger in this world of commonplace,
'Cause if waft by lofty hopes you'll be mocked and put to shame.

75 And so, my friend, why my good pen rusts in the ink you must not ask
Nor why verse has lost its power to tempt me from the daily task,
Nor why I sleep my days away, with crushed in yellow pages there
Climbing iambus, trochees swift, and dactyl with the sprightly air.
If I should further write, I fear my good contemporaries might laud,
80 Perhaps, my name in verse, and with their praise my work reward;
And if to now I have endured their hatred with a smiling face,
Such praise would seem to me indeed a truly measureless disgrace.

SATIRE III

A Sultan among those who over a language reign,
Who where the flocks are pastured, there stretches their domain,
Was sleeping on the hillside, his head laid on his arm,
When came to him a vision that did his spirit charm:
5   He saw the moon that nightly across the heavens ranged
Turn from her wonted journey and to a maiden changed,
He saw her glide towards him, with lovely downcast head,
And there was sorrow in her eyes; but spring bloomed at her tread;
While all the forest trembled, so wondrous was her grace,
10   And a thrill of silver ripples ran o'er the water's face.
A mist like sparkling diamonds that did the vision daze
Lay on the earth enchanted, a bright illumined haze,
While the sound of whispered music sang through that wonderland,
And o'er the starry heavens a midnight rainbow spanned . . .
15   Her hair in raven tresses about her shoulders fell,
And taking his hand in hers, she these grave words did tell:
"Let be our lives united, my pain let yours enfold
That through your sorrow's sweetness my sorrow be consoled . . .
Writ was it through the ages and all the stars record
20   That I shall be your mistress, and you shall be my lord."
Now, as the Sultan marvelled, softly she withdrew
And he felt as if within him a wondrous tree upgrew;
A tree that in an instant raised loftily its head
And to the far horizons its thrusting branches spread;
25   A tree of such a stature that even at midday
The farthest lands and oceans under its shadow lay.

While at the earth's four corners rose up against the sky
Atlas, Caucasus, Taurus and the Balkan mountains high;
The wide Euphrates, Tigris, the Nile, the Danube old,
30   All 'neath its boughs protecting their mighty waters rolled.
Asia, Europe, Africa and the desert stretching far,
The boats that on the lakes and seas and on the rivers are,
Billowing, boundless corn-fields that tossed emerald locks,
And shores, and ships, and harbours with castles on the rocks,
35   All these spread like a carpet his vision did embrace,
Country next to country set, and race to race . . .
All these as in a mist of silver did he see,
A vast extending kingdom' neath the shadow of a tree.

The eagle that aspires the sky does dawdle not
40 |With lazy wings, nor in among the branches squat;
And now a wind of conquest the ancient forest fills
And shouts of Allah! Allah! echo among the hills,
As though a rising tempest does o'er the ocean roar
The deafening clash of battle, the thunderous clang of war;
45 |Till loudly does the forest to that great gale resound.
And bow before new Rome its branches to the ground.

The Sultan then awakened to find the moon again
Her wonted place had taken above Eskishehr plain,
And sadly to the dwelling of Sheik Edebali turned
50   And through the window bars a girlish form discerned,
More lithesome than a hazel, a maid who gravely smiled,
Sweet Malcatun the beautiful, Sheik Edebali's child.
And then it was he understood his dream sent by the prophet,
As though a moment he had gained the presence of Mahomet;
55   He knew that born of this his love would there an empire grow
Of which the tides and boundaries only the sky would know.

Now, as the eagle rises the Sultan's dream came true,
And year by year invincible that gathering kingdom grew,

And year by year the emerald flame flew higher in the blast
60　As generations came and went and as each sultan passed;
Nor was there any nation could its course forbid
Until up to the Danube rode conquering Bayazid.
From one bank to the other a bridge of boats was cast
And all that host marched over midst fanfare trumpet blast,
65　The bodyguard of Allah did over the Danube ride
Darkening with their numbers the Rovine countryside,
Swarming tens of thousands spreading their tents immense;
But on the far horizon stood oaks in forest dense.

Now came a company of men, in front a white flag borne,
70　And Bayazid regarding them enquired with haughty scorn:
"What do you want?"
　　　　"We want but peace, and if it be allowed
Our Sire would like to speak awhile with you, great Sultan proud."

At a sign the way was cleared, and came towards the tent
75　A man of calm and simple mien, and with the years bent.
'Is't Mircea?"
　　　　"Yes your Highness!"
　　　　　　　　"Take heed, for caution warns,
Lest you your crown exchange against a wreath of thorns."
80　"That you have come, great emperor, no heed what be your aim,
While still at peace I hail you, our greetings that you came;
But, as to your good council, o may the Lord forgive,
If you do dream to win this land by force imperative;
Had you not better return home with calm and peaceful mind
85　And show in your imperial strength that you are just and kind...
Be the one or be the other, but little does it awe,
Gladly shall we take our fare, either peace or war."
"What, when nations open their gates before my trump
You think my hosts will stumble against a rotten stump?
90　You do not guess, old dotard, the force my foes deployed.

160

The West's most noble flower these soldiers have destroyed.
O'er all the cross does shelter, emperors and kings,
The crescent moon ascending its silver shadow flings.
Aye, clad in gleaming armour the cavaliers of Malta,
95   The Pope who wears three crowns and guards the Holy Altar
Lightning against lightning set and thunder against thunder,
A storm that fraught the sea with fear and filled the earth with wonder
I needed but to make a sign, a movement of my head
And all the nations in my path in wild disorder fled;
100 For strong to overthrow the cross did march a mighty host
O'er sea its rule from land to land, on land from coast to coast;
Shattering the peace of earth as it did march along,
Darkening the countryside in tens of thousand strong.
Our lances stood uncounted like a field of growing corn,
105 And tremble did the ocean o'er which our ships were borne.
At Nicopolis you no doubt saw how many camps were brought,
As though a shining metall wall of swords and spears wrought.
But when I saw their number like the leaves and like the grass,
I swore that I would crush them down and through their midst would
                                                          pass;
110 I swore that I would scatter them as wind upflings the foam,
And give my charger hay and oast in the Vatican at Rome ...
Yet you before my legions imagine you can stand,
You ridiculous old dotard, with a bare staff in your hand?"
"To that old dotard, Emperor, aught one courtesy accord
115 For over all Wallachia 'tis he the chosen lord.
And wiser you would guard your words, nor yet too loudly boast,
Lest should the furious Danube flood engulf your fleeing host.
Along the rollihg ages many there were who came
Since Darius Hystaspis of tall immortal fame;
120 Many there were who flung their dream across the Danube's tide
And set their bridges ship to ship and over them did ride;
Emperors unnumbered, for their cruelty renowned,
Who came to us with hungry eyes for water and for ground;
And though I would not care to brag, tell you this thing I must:
125 Little time went by ere they were water and were dust.

You boast that on your conquering road no gates for long were closed
Though all the flower the of West your vanguard's march opposed;
But what the high aspiring cause that did their hearts endure?
The vanity of every brave, of every cavalier;
130 The pomp of noisy conquest; for they had set their vow
To tear the pride from out your heart, the laurels from your brow.
But I defend the poverty and the needs of a struggling land
And therefore all the rocks and streams and hills that guardian stand
And all that grows and moves and breathes to me is ally true,
135 While every blade of grass and stone is enemy to you;
We have small hosts, yet love of soil had ever power to rid
This flowering land of all its foes. Prepare then Bayazid!"

No sooner had he gone than mighty the commotion!
The forest rang with arms, and rumbled like the ocean,
140 Amidst the greenwood thousand heads with long and plaited hair,
And sev'ral thousands more besides that did bright helmets wear.
While wave on wave of cavalry over the plain did flood
Astride high prancing chargers, their stirrups carved of wood.
Thundering over the battered earth an avalanche they went,
145 Lances levelled to the charge and bows near double bent;
Till like a shower of shivering light that whistled through the air,
A storm of arrows leapt and sang and flew from everywhere;
A din of blows on armour dealt like rattling of hail,
The noise of hoof and sword and lance, the roar of battle gale.
150 Unheeded was the Emperor's fury, lion-like his rage,
For hotter still about his troops the fight did deadly wage;
Unheeded did the green flame flutter o'er his stricken ranks
For mightily assailed in front, attacked on both their flanks,
The East's entire battle host was scattered in the fray
155 And line on line of infantry mown down like summer hay.
A steady rain of arrows fell and sword blows did resound,
While riders dropped on every hand and dead bestrewed the ground.
Till, onset from all sides at once, helpless to fight or fly,
It seemed the very earth was doomed and fallen was the sky . . .

160 Mircea himself led on his men midst storm of battle lust
    That came, and came, and came, that trod all in the dust;
    Their cavalry undaunted, a wall of lances proud
    Which through that pagan army streets of daylight ploughed
    And laid to earth their thousands like sheafs of ripened corn,
165 High in the van of conquest Wallachia's banner borne;
    As deluge flung from heaven that burst upon the seas,
    Till in an hour the heathen were chaff before the breeze
    And from that hail of iron fast towards the Danube fled,
    While gloriously behind them th'Romanian army spread.

170 Now, while the troops are camping, the sun goes slowly down
    Decking the lofty summits with victory's gold crown;
    The lightning that from terror had flown out of the sky
    Now flashes forth its splendour along the mountains high,
    While gradually the planets do up the heaven rear
175 And o'er the mist-drenched forest the pallid moon appear,
    The queen of night and ocean that squanders calm and sleep.
    Yet of the sons of Mircea does one still vigil keep,
    And on his knee, in musing, beneath the evening star,
180 He writes to his beloved of Argeş village far:
            "From deep within Rovine vale,
            O lady fair, we bid you hail,
            Alas, by letter not by speech,
            By sundering distance out of reach.
185   Yet am I fain to beg of thee
            To send by messenger to me
            What in your valley fairest be:
            The forest with its silver glade,
            Thy eyes that long, curl'd lashes shade.
190   And I in turn will send to you
            The proudest thing that here we view:
            This mighty host with banner spread,
            The forest, branching overhead,
            My helmet with its feathery crest,

195 My eyes that 'neath their lashes rest.
I have both health and resting-place,
Thanks be to Christ and to God's grace,
And now, dear love, I thee embrace".

. . . .
. . . .
. . . .
. . . .

By such an age as this were chroniclers inspired;
200 But our good age of mountebanks what poet's heart has fired...
In annals of past ages heroes are often found,
But poet, with your late or lyre of dreaming sound
Have you a single patriot to sing about today?
Apollo at the sight of these had hid himself away!
205 O modern heroes squatting beneath far glory's wing,
Since you are all the fashion I would your prowess sing;
While draped in perfect nullity your praise is writ by those
Who knead the golden ages within the mud of prose.
Muşats and *Basarabs* rest in your sacred shade,
210 Givers of law and justice, men who our nation made,
Who with the mace and ploughshare spread out our boundaries wide
From seashore to the mountains, and to the Danube side.

The *present* is not noble? Calling for heroes we?
Is not our street quite famous for dealers in jewelry?
215 Have not in far Sybaris our manners gained first prize?
From tavern door and alley does glory not arise?
And have we then no heroes, who wield rhetoric slings
Amidst the noisy plaudit of hordes of gutterings?
These pickpockets of honour who on a tightrope dance,
220 And wear their fancy costumes with perfect elegance.
Of *Virtue* and *The Nation* our liberal prates, till sure
His daily life you'd fancy must be as crystal pure?
You'd never dream him being a cafe haunting knave,

Who mocks at his own sermon, so solemn, and so grave.
225 O could you see the brigand that no conscience has nor soul
With his hang-dog expression and heavy, sullen jaw,
A hunchback, evil-visaged, a spring of cunning greed,
Who spouts out for his comrades some poisoned, nonsense creed.
Upon each lip is Virtue, and in each heart deceit;
230 A set of wicked monsters and wrong from head to feet
Who round their patrons standing, as those who Gods admire,
Will roll protruding frog eyes, bright with their hearts' aspire.
Such men become our leaders, its laws' our country give,
Men who at best from kindness should in a madhouse live
235 Clothed each in madmen's jackets, a fool's cap on each head.
But no . . . they teach us wisdom and make our laws instead.
Patriotism ! Justice ! . . . Such guardians of our State
Despise the laws as nonsense that they themselves create.
As sly as artful foxes will they the benches throng
240 Frenetically applauding our country game and song;
Then meeting in the Senate each others praises speak
This heavy-throated Bulgar, that long and hook-nosed Greek.
Each claims to be Romanian, whatever mask he wears,
These Bulgo-Greeks pretending that they are Trajan's heirs;
245 This poison froth, this dung-heap, this foul and filthy brood
Have they indeed inherited our nation's masterhood !
The scourings of everywhere, the abortive and the maimed,
All that man rejected and nature has disclaimed,
These crafty, greedy gluttons, these grasping Phanariots
250 To us they all have flooded and pose as patriots.
Until at last these nothings, this foul and loathful scum,
These cripple-minded stammerers lords of our land become.

Are you then Rome's descendants, you eunuchs and no men?
If you were men in earnest, pity it were that then
255 This hungry plague of locusts, these creatures crazed and lame
Dare part their lips in public and flatter without shame
Our nation's majesty, and make it odious stand,
Dare even speak thy name . . . o miserable land !

In Paris pleasure houses, there has your congress been;
260 With jaded, worthless women, in revelry obscene,
In sloth and vulgar rioting you wasted wealth and youth;
In you what could develop, that empty are in sooth?

And, coming back, for wisdom a perfume flask you brought,
A monocle you flourished, a cane for sword you bought.
265 Withered up before your time, yet childish in your brain,
For scientific knowledge a Bal-Mabil refrain,
And all your father's riches spent on some harlot's shoe:
O admirable and worthy offspring of Romans, you!
And now just look with horror on faces sceptic cold,
270 What wonder that your falsehoods no more persuasion hold?
When those who speak fine phrases and lofty sermons give
Would simply fill their pockets, that they may lazy live,
Today the polished discourse does little credence know,
But others are the reasons, dear Sirs, is that not so?
275 Too much have you made riches and power your single aim,
Too much have brought our nation to ridicule and shame,
Too much you mocked the language and customs of this race,
That now at last your mocking does but yourselves disgrace,
While self was e'er the craving that in your spirits stirred,
280 Genius? A nonsense. Virtue? But a word.

O, leave in the old chronicles our forefathers to rest;
For they would gaze upon you with irony at best.
Rise once more, o Ţepeş! Take and divide these men
As lunatics and rogues in two big tribes, and then
285 In mighty, twin infirmaries by force both tribes intern,
And with a single faggot prison and madhouse burn.

SATIRE IV

See the tall and lonely castle mirrored in the placid lake,
'Neath those waters does its shadow through the ages never wake,
Silently above the pine-tress rise its ancient rampart stark,
Throwing wide a flood of shadow o'er the brooding waters dark.
5 Through the high and arched windows silver curtains one can see,
Like the hoar frost coldly shining, hanging folds of drapery.
Slowly climbing up the heavens shows the moon behind the pines,
And the rocky crags and tree tops on the silver sky designs,
While the mighty oaks encircling like a watching giant band
10 Round, as though around some treasure, silent guard of honour stand.
Only the white swans that slowly through the rushes take their way,
Emperors of that lonely water, hold their pround and silent sway,
Now, as though to mount the heavens, spreading wide their mighty
wings

Do they beat the water's surface, breaking it in silver rings,
15 While the sleeping rushes shiver giving forth a secret sigh
And in the flower-sprinkled grass does a criket sound its cry;
There's sweet sound and so much scent and so much summer in the air ...

Beneath the hidden balcony a lonely knight is standing there,
The balcony hung o'er with leaves, in clusters round its pillars twined
20 Roses of Shiraz in bloom, and creeping plants of diverse kind;
While he intoxicated by the breeze that off the sleeping water strays
Amidst fair nature's magic spell on his guitar a nocturn plays.

"Beloved, show thyself again in thy long flowing silken gown
Which clinging close about thee seems with silver dust to be weighed
down.

25 My whole life would I gaze on thee, that dost a crown of radiance wear
When thou dost lift thy small white hand to smooth aside thy golden hair.
Come sport with me ... and with my luck ... throw from thy casement
in the skies

A little faded meadow flower that on thy swelling bosom lies,
So that in falling it may strike on my guiter a trembling sound.
30 So bright the darkness it does seem that silver snow lies on the ground.
If to the perfumed fastness of your curtained boudoir I might win
Intoxicated with the scent of snowy flaxen sheets within,
Cupid, that small bantering page, would hide between his hands the
⎰flame

Of thy bright gleaming bedside lamp, my beauteous, my graceful dame !"
35 A gentle sound of rustling silk ... a form that moves the leaves between
Among the scarlet roses and the climbing deep blue creepers seen.
Among the flowers the maiden laughs, and leans her hand the bars
above —

Sweet as the image of a saint the faces are of those that love —
She throws him down a crimson rose, then on her lips a finger lays
40 As though to chide him, yet the while soft whispered words of passion
says.

Then drawing back she disappears ... sound of steps that come in haste ...
And through the door she slips at last, the knight has ta'en her round
the waist

And arm in arm they stride away ... a pretty match they make withall'
So lovely she, and he so young, and both of them so slim and tall.
45 Out of the shadow of the cliff, towards the open shining lake,
With loose and lazy flapping sails, their boat its gentle course does take
And slowly through the silver night, amid the sound of lapping oars,
They glide across a magic lake that lies between enchanted shores.

The moon now, to her fullness come, athwart the sky her lantern swings
50 And o'er the water, shore to shore, a path of silver brilliance flings

That she upon the ripples lays, as though by lips of fairies kissed,
She, the child of heaven's clear, dream of everlasting mist.
Gradually her beam grows brighter, clearer still and still more clear,
While the farther hills upstanding in her gleam quite close appear,
55 Wider too the forest growing that does clothe the water's side,

Spreading 'neath the disc of heaven, Queen of all that shining tide.
The while, tall limes with shadows wide, their blossoms trailing to the
ground,
Above the shady waters lean and through their leaves soft breezes sound,
While on the maiden's golden head many scented petals light.
60 Now does she place her slender hands about the neck of that fair knight

And, raising up her face to his, tenderly she whispers this:
"Deep in my soul how wildly sweet the word upon thy red lip is.
And oh, to what a heaven high within thy mind thou lift thy slave,
Still is the yearning in thy heart the single happiness I have.
65 And with its gentle fire thy voice can hurt and fill my soul with fears,

For ours does seem a tale of love passed down to us from bygone years.
A wondrous unspoken dream thy eyes that do so sadly yearn,
Within their humid, thirsty depths I am consumed and ever burn.
O, give me back your gleaming eyes and turn them not away from me,
70 An ever standing miracle shall their eternal darkness be,

Fain would I gaze till I grow blind beholding them. But listen now
How countless tress and ripples soft hold converse with the stars, and how
The woods with dark delirious joy are full, and how the azure springs
Speak to each other of our love amid their happy babblings,
75 While Lucifer is trembling midst the summits of the highest trees,

The whole wide earth, the lake, the sky, all are our accomplices.
Well may we loose the rudder and let the lazy oars lie still
That on the water's gentle breast the waves should bear us where they will,
No matter where the waters drive, no matter what the kind wind's
breath,
80 For everywhere our joy will lie ... little matter life or death."

. . . .

Fany, naught but fancy's farce. Whene'er we are alone we two,

How oft you take me on the lake, what seas and forests guide
me through!
Where did you see these unknown lands of which you speak to me
today?
And where these joys? Since then I deem five hundred years
have passed away.
85   Today one may not loose one's soul enchanted by a maiden's gaze,
Though sick with longing you may be, you will not gain such maiden's
ways,
As with your arms about her neck, with mouth to mouth and breast
to breast,
Her eyes are asking: "Tell me true, 'tis really me you love the best?"
Alas, your hand is scarce held out but op'ns the door and pour in
through
90   A swarm of wretched relatives, some uncles, then an aunt or two.
You hang your head, grin bashfully, and silent ask the skies above
If there be not in all the world a quiet spot in which to love.
Like mummies brought from Egypt they, stiffly upright in their chairs,
While you with twisting fingers writhe, numbering your moustache's
hairs,
95   Or roll unwanted cigarettes, or sit with clenched and folded hands
And show how sensible you are, who even cooking understands.

O, I am weary of a life composed of disillusion's stuff,
Of misery and bitter prose ... of such a life I've had enough;
To hallow with so many tears an instinct so banal and vain,
100   An instinct that the birds have got, and every spring comes back again.
You do not live, another soul inspires you, lives in your stead,
Laughs with your mouth, is happy. He, and he it was who whispered.
Your lives are like the ripples which into oblivion run away,
Eternity is evil all, and sin, a demigod, holds sway.
105   Do you not realize your love is not your own, you madman you?
Do you not know what nonsense cheap you hold for marvels and are
true?

Do you not realize that love is only one of nature's needs?

Do you not know it nurtures lives that have in them but Satan's seeds?
Do you not see your laughter is the source of your own children's
tears?
110 Cain's influence is on the earth and still no end to it appears.
O, theatre of puppet plays full of the babble of mankind . . .
Like parrots, they a thousand jokes and endless nonsense tales unwind.
Yet understand they not at all the things they tell. An actor climbs
Upon the stage and tells himself again, again ten thousand times,
115 What every age has always said, what every age will always say
Until the sun dips in the sea upon the eve of judgement day.
O, do you dream when midst the clouds the moon her nihgtly course
does steer.
Dream deep in your imagined world that you your maiden can ender?
At midnight wander through the snow along a frosty wind-swept road
120 And gaze through lighted windows at the lighted rooms of her abode?
You'd see her stand complacently with many a worthless waiting beau
There gathered round, and each in turn a little winsome ogle throw,
Hear clank of spurs, see silken gowns from which faint rustling murmurs
rise,
The young men turn mustachios, the ladies rolling sheeplike eyes.
125 While she with amorous glance accepts their propositions at her ease,
You, with your stupid sentiments, would you before her doorway freeze?
O passionate and stubborn fool, to love her in this childish way
When she is cold and whimsical, and sudden as an April day.
You clasp together longing hands, a madman's dream does you enthral,
130 For you would take her in your arms, to have her and to hold her all,
As though a Parian marble fair, or canvas that Correggio wrought,
Cold and coquettish as she is. Believe me, 'tis a foolish thought.
Aye, the maiden I had dreamt of, who would of love's enchantment know,
Who when I sat enwrapt in thought would lean upon my shoulder so
135 That I would feel her presence near, and know I understood at last
To make of living but a tale, a life in happy legend past.
I seek no more. What should I seek? The same old song of my desire,
The hunger for eternal peace that sets my wretched soul afire.
The silver chords are broken now, my lyre no more of love does sing,
140 And yet the ancient song I hear sometimes at nicht beside the spring

171

Where, here and there, amidst the dark, a gleam of milk-white
moonlight strays
From out a *Carmen saeculare* as I did dream in former days...
But for this sad sigh and wailing, whistling, discordant sound,
Scattered cries and tangled noises in my weeping lyre are found.
145   Through my mind a breeze of winter sadly is a journey wending,
And around me chants forever tale of time inept unending.

What the outcome of existence? Where the message that I had?
All the lyre's chords are broken, and the minstrel man is mad.

LUCIFER

Once on a time, as poets sing
    High tales with fancy laden,
Born of a very noble king
    There lived a wondrous maiden.

5 An only child, her kinsfolk boon,
    So fair, imagination faints;
As though amidst the stars the moon,
    Or Mary amidst the saints.

From 'neath the castle's dark retreat,
10   Her silent way she wended
Each evening to the window-seat
    Where Lucifer attended.

    And secretly, with never fail,
She watched his double race,
15   Where vessels drew their pathless trail
Across the ocean's face.

And as intent she drank his light,
    Desire was quickly there;
While he who saw her every night
20   Soon fell in love with her.

And sitting thus with rested head,
    Her elbows on the sill,
Her heart by youthful fancy led
    Did with deep longing fill.

25 While he, a brilliant shining spark,
    Glowed always yet more clear
Towards the castle tall and dark
    Where she would soon appear

* * *

Until one night with shower of rays
30   He slips into her room,
As though a strange and silver haze
    Did round about her loom.

And when at last the child to rest
    Upon her sofa lies,
35 He lays her arms acroos her breast
    And closes her soft eyes.

While where his ray on mirror lands
    And is upon her couch redrifted,
It falls upon her throat and hands
40   And on her face uplifted.

A smile is on her lips it seems;
    He in the mirror trembles,
For smooth his ray glides midst her dreams
    And round her soul assembles.

45 And while she is in slumber gone
    She murmurs through her sighs:
"Come down to me beloved one,
    Fair prince of the clear skies.

Come down, good Lucifer and kind,
50   O lord of my aspire,
And flood my chamber and my mind
    With your sweetest fire !"

And Lucifer beams still more bright
    To hear her word's emotion;
55 Then like a comet in its flight
    Dives down into the ocean.

And where his bolt is lost to view
    The sea in whirlpool surges,
Till out of the unfathomed blue
60   A handsome youth emerges,

Who, leaping off the fretful wave,
    Lightly through her casement passes;
And in his hand he holds a stave
    Crowned with a wreath of grasses.

65 A prince indeed of royal stock,
    With heavy hanging golden hair;
A purple winding-sheet his smock,
    Hung round his shoulders bare.

A starry glow shines from his eyes,
70   His cheeks are deathly white;
A lifeless thing in living guise,
    A youth born of the night.

"Down from the spheres do I come
    Though dreadful the commotion,
75 My father is the vaulted dome,
    My mother is the ocean.

For I have left my realm to keep
        Obedience to your command;
Born of the zenith and the deep
80   Here I before you stand.

O come, fair child of roya birth,
        Cast this your world aside,
For Lucifer has flown to earth
        To claim you as his bride.

85 And you will live till time is done
        In castles built of sky,
And all the fish will be your own,
        And all the birds that fly".

"O, beautiful you are, good Sire,
90   As but an angel prince could be,
But to the course that you desire
        I never shall agree

Strange, as your voice and vesture show,
        I live while you are dead;
95 Your eyes gleam with an icy glow
        Which fills my soul with dread."

* * *

One day went past, and went past two,
        Then o'er the castle dark,
Fair Lucifer again to view
100   Shone forth his lustrious spark.

And scarce his beam waved bright above,
        Her dreams to him were borne,
Her heart again by aching love
        And cruel longing torn.

105 "Come down, good Lucifer and kind,
    O lord of my aspire,
And flood my chamber and my mind
    With your sweetest fire !"

    Now, as he heard her tender cry
110   With pain he faded out,
And lightning flew about the sky,
    Which wheeled and rocked about;

Around the earth a lurid glow
    Poured like a torrent race,
115 Till out of its chaotic flow
    There grew a human face;

About the head dark wisps of hair
    Girt with a crown of flame,
And through the sun-illumined air
120   Borne up by truth he came.

His arms of rounded marble sheen
    Did 'neath a cloak of raven show,
And sad and thoughtful was his mien
    And pallid was his brow.

125 Bright eyes he had that seem'd to tell
    Of strange chimeric bonds;
And deep they were as passion's spell,
    And dark as moonlit ponds.

"Down from the spheres have I flown,
130   Though terrible my flight;
My father wears Apollo's crown,
    My mother is the night.

O come, fair child of royal birth,
    Cast this your world aside,
135 For Lucifer has flown to earth
      To claim you as his bride.

A starry halo from the skies
    About your hair will fall,
And you among the spheres will rise
140   The proudest of them all."

"O, beautiful you are, good Sire,
    As but a demon prince could be,
But to the course of your desire
    I never shall agree.

145 You wound me with your crude behest;
    I dread what you extol;
Your heavy eyes, as though possessed,
    Gleam down into my soul."

,,But why should I descend to thee?
150   Far better what I give;
My days are all eternity,
    While you but one hour live."

"I would not chosen phrases seek,
    Nor carefully my words arrange,
155 But though with human mouth you speak,
    Your speech to me is strange.

Yet if you wish to prove your worth,
    That I betroth myself to you,
Well, then come down to me on earth
160   And be a mortal too."

"You ask my endless life above
　　To barter for a kiss.
Aye, I will show how my love,
　　How deep my longing is.

165　My birthright I will fling aside
　　To be reborn of sin, and I
Who to all rolling time am tied,
　　Will that great knot untie."

At which he turned and went away
170　　Midst a cloud of sombre pearl,
To renounce his birthright from that day
　　For the love of a mortal girl.

* * *

About this time young Cătălin
　　Was a page boy of that house,
175 Who filled the festive cups with wine
　　At feast and royal carouse.

And carried high the regal train;
　　A foundling, brought by chance,
Born of a humble unknown strain,
180　　Though roguish in his glance,

Round-cheeked, like rose-apples red,
　　Mischievous, bright-eyed,
He slipped with quick yet stealthy tread
　　To Cătălina's side.

185 Upon my soul, Queen of romance!
　　Was such a darling ever?
Come Cătălin, quick try your chance,
　　For now's your time or never.

At which he round her waist did twine
190   His arm in sudden wooing.
"Behave, you rascal Cătălin,
     Whatever are you doing?"

"By sorrow brooding all the while
     You would your heart assuage,
195 But better you would turn and smile
     And kiss just once your page."

"I know not what your wishes are,
     Leave me alone, you knave.
Ah me ! The longing for that star
200   Will drive me to the grave."

"If you don't know, and you would learn
     How love is set about,
Don't recklessly my teaching spurn,
     First fairly hear me out.

205 As trappers deftly birds pursue
     With nets among the tree,
When I stretch out my arm to you,
     Slip your arm thus round me.

Your eyes into my eyes must glow,
210   Nor turn away, nor close
And when I lift you softly, so,
     Rise gently on your toes.

And when my face is downwards bent
     Your face turned up will stay,
215 That we may gaze with sweet intent
     For ever and a day.

While should you wish at last to learn
    The measure of love's bliss,
When hot my lips on yours do burn
220   Give back again my kiss."

Amused, yet with a girl's surprise
    At what the youth acclaimed,
She blushed and turned away her eyes,
    Half willing, half ashamed.

225 "A chatterbox you were since small
    With overmuch to tell,
Yet I had felt, in spite of all,
    We'd suit each other well".

But Lucifer's slow sailing spark
230   Crept up out of the sea
Over the horizon's arc,
    Prince of eternity.

And now my wretched heart does bleed,
    With tears my eyes grow dim,
235 Whene'er I watch the waves that speed
    Across the sea to him.

While he looms with adoring ray
    My grief to overthrow,
Yet ever climbs to heights away
240   Where mortals cannot go.

His silver beams that space defy
    Sadly my watchers are
And I shall love him till I die,
    Yet he be ever far.

245 And thus it is the days to me
   Are drear as desert sand,
The nights filled with a mystery
   I dare not understand . . ."

 "How childish is the way you speak.
250   Come on ! Come, lets run away,
That all the world for us shall seek
   Though no one finds the way.

And we shall nothing of this life regret
   But joyous live and sprightly,
255 Till soon your parents you'll forget,
   Nor dream your longings nightly."

* * *

Lucifer set out and o'er
   The sky his wings extended,
And million years flew past before
260   As many moments ended.

A sky of stars above his way,
   A sky of stars below;
As lightning flash midst them astray
   In one continuous flow.

265 Till round his primal chaos hurled
   When out of causeless night
The first, upflaming dawn unfurled
   Its miracle of light.

Still further flew he ere the start
270   Of things of form devoid,
Spurred by the yearning of his heart,
   Far back into the void.

Yet where he reach's is not the bourn
    Nor yet where eye can see;
275 Beyound where struggling time was torn
    Out of eternity.

Around him there was naught. And still,
    Strange yearning there was yet,
A yearning that all space did fill,
280   As when the blind forget.

"O, Father God, this knot untie
    Of my celestial birth,
And praised you will be on high
    And on the rolling earth.

285 The price you ask is little count,
    Give fate another course,
For you are of fair life the fount
    And of calm death the source.

Take back this halo from my head,
290   Take back my starry lower,
And give to me, o God, instead
    Of human love one hour.

Out of the chaos was I wrought,
    In chaos would I be dispersed,
295 Out of the empty darkness brought,
    For darkness do I thirst..."

"Hyperion, o child divine,
    Don't thus your state disclaim,
Nor ask for miracle, nor sign
300   That has nor sense nor name.

You wish to be of man a son,
　　To be a star you scorn;
But men quick perish every one,
　　And men each day are born.

305　Yet stars burn on with even glow,
　　And it is fate's intending
That they nor time, nor place shall know,
　　Unfettered and unending.

　　Out of eternal yesterday
310　　Into tomorrow's grave,
Even the sun will pass way
　　That other sun's shall lave;

The sun that every morn does rise
　　At last it's spirit gives;
315　For each thing lives because it dies,
　　And dies because it lives.

But you, Hyperion, never wane,
　　Night's miracle sublime,
But in the sky your place retain,
320　　The wonder of all time.

So what strange fancy holds your mind?
　　What dreaming thus belates you?
Return to earth and there you'll find
　　The awakening that awaits you."

*　*　*

325　Hyperion did straightway go
　　To where through ages gone
His gleam upon the earth below
　　Nightly he had shone.

And it was evening when he came,
330   Night's darkness slow assembled,
And rose the moon a frozen flame
      That in the water trembled,

And filled the forest's twilight clime
      With a silver starry mist,
335 Where 'neath a tall and spreading lime
      Two fair-haired children kissed.

"O, let me lay in lover's wise
      My head upon your breast,
Beneath the wonder of your eyes,
340   In soft and fragrant rest.

In mystery's enchanted light
      Pervade me with your charm,
And flood my soul through passion's night
      With time's eternal calm.

345 O, quench my longing's eager thirst,
      My aching doubts o'ercast,
For you to me are love the first,
      And of my dreams the last."

Hyperion gazed down and knew
350   The fire their souls possessed;
For scarce the boy her nearer drew,
      She clasped him to her breast.

A rain of petals in the air
      That softly did enfold
355 Two fervent children strangely fair,
      With locks of plated gold.

She, lost in love's enraptured flight,
    To heaven turned her eyes,
Saw Lucifer's down shining light
360   And whispered through her sighs:

"Come down, good Lucifer and kind,
    O lord of my aspire.
And fill the forest and my mind
    With your sweetest fire!"

365 And Lucifer, alone in space,
    Her tender summons heard,
A planet o'er the ocean's face
    That trembled at her word,

But did not plunge as'n former day,
    And in his heart did cry:
370 "O, what care you, fair face of clay,
    If it be he or I?

Still earth shall only earth remain,
    Let luck its course unfold,
375 And I in my own kingdom reign
    Immutable and cold."

TO THE CRITICS

Many the buds that come to flower,
Though to bear fruit scarce any at all;
Youth beats on the gates of blooming,
Yet how many blossoms fall.

5 It is easy to write verses
When you have not what to tell,
Stringing words and hollow phrases
In a gangling doggerel.

But the day one's heart is flooded,
10 Yearnings deep and passions dear,
Truth that speaks a thousand voices,
How should one to each give ear?

Like the buddings at life's gateway
Thoughts beat eager on the mind,
15 Claiming loud to life an entrance,
Claiming being of mankind.

How then when upspringing passion,
Wild emotions in one rise,
How should one find sober judgement?
20 How retain impassive eyes?

Ah, one feels that then in thunder
Round one's head the heavens roll;
How should man find true expression
To describe his teeming soul?

25 Citics, you of sterile blossom,
Where's the fire that in you stirred?
It is easy to write verses
Out of nothing but the word.

HOW MANY A STAR BURNS...

How many a star burns in the firmament,
How many a wave the sea before her throws,
Gleaming and sparkling fair, yet no man knows
What may their meaning be, or their intent.

5   Thus, you may choose the way your footsteps went;
High or low though be the path you chose,
The selfsame dust, the selfsame earth will close
Your heritage in time's oblivion spent.

I seem to die, and near the shadowed gate,
10 With funeral dirge and flickering tapers set,
The men who are to bear my body wait.

O, pleasant shade, come near, come nearer yet,
That I may know thee, lord of death's estate,
With tall black wings and drooping lashes wet.

SO LONG, DEAR ONE, SINCE YOU DEPARTED...
(Except)

So long, dear one, since you departed,
Since last we spoke it is so long,
I feel as though I had forgotten
How our love was blind and strong.

5 Today again you sit before me;
Pallidly, yet e'er so sweet...
Let me now, as I was wonted,
Kneel down humbly at your feet.

Let me weep for you my pity,
10 Kiss your fingers one by one.
O little hands, my own beloved,
Through all these weeks what have you done?

HIGH O'ER THE MAIN

High o'er the main
Many stars beaming,
Distantly gleaming
    Thus till they wane.

5   Thunderous stroke
Of green billows breaking,
Creaking and quacking
    Great vessels of oak.

Like castles far blown
10   Adrift on the ocean,
Ever in motion,
    Ever alone.

Herons migrating
Pass o'er the sky,
15   Hurrying by,
    And never waiting.

Fly till they fall,
Yet others starting,
Eternally parting . . .
20   Aye, that is all.

Blossoms the rose,
But life has swift flowers
And youth like the hours
    Scarce comes than it goes.

25   Thus every delight,
No matter its reasons,
Is swept by the seasons
    Soon out of our sight.

O angels above,
30 While I am still here
To my singing give ear,
    To my sadness and love.

For shame is it not
Thus to squander scarce seeing
35 This moment of being
    That is all we have got?

OF ALL THE SHIPS

Of all the ships the ocean rolls
    How many find untimely graves
Piled high by you upon the shoals,
    O waves and winds, o winds and waves?

5 How many a bird that leaves its bower
    And o'er the sky in autumn draves
You beat and blindly overpower,
    O waves and winds, o winds and waves?

Should easy luck or high endeavour
10   Be our aim it little saves,
For you pursue our footsteps ever,
    O waves and winds, o winds and waves.

Still, it is past our comprehending
    What design your song enslaves,
15 Rolling on until time's ending,
    O waves and winds, o winds and waves.

DIANA

What do you seek where moon is spending
Her bright glow on trembling spring,
And the birds a song unending
In among the branches sing?
5 Don't you hear amid the dingle
How the leaves with whispers sweet
Softly kiss and intermingle
Through the forest's cool retreat?

In what moving mirror showing
10 Have you watched the ripples play,
When the water's endless flowing
'Neath your gaze its course did stay?
In each sound new life is teeming,
May has from the forest gone,
15 Only you are wonder dreaming
Like the youthful Endymion.

Why do you so lonely wander,
Hark the spring's small secret sound?
Fall asleep where tall tress squander
20 Their green carpet on the ground?
Through the woods with twilight laden
Ripples cool and shadows there,
Do you wait a fairy maiden
With big eyes and shoulders bare?

25 Ah! Amid the branches bending,
    Hands of snow that part the glade,
    Softly through the woodland wending,
    Lonely, lithesome, lovely maid,
    On her back a golden quiver,
30 To the chase her path does wind,
    And upon the leaves a shiver,
    Scarce a footprint leaves behind.

'TIS EVE ON THE HILLSIDE

'Tis eve on the hillside, the bagpipes are distantly wailing,
Flocks going homewards, and stars o'er the firmament sailing,
Sound of the bubbling spring sorrow's legend narrating,
And beneath a tall willow for me, dear one, you are waiting.

5   The wandering moon up the heavens her journey is wending,
Big-eyed you watch through the boughs her gold lantern ascending,
Now over the dome of the sky all the planets are gleaming,
And heavy your breast with its longing, your brow with its dreaming,

Corn-fields bright flooded with beams by the clouds steeply drifted,
10 Old cottage gables of thatch to the moonlight uplifted,
The tall wooden arm of the well in the wind softly grating,
And the shepherd-boy's pipe from the sheep-pen sad *doina* relating.

The peasants, their scythes on their backs, from their labour are coming.
The sound of the *toaca* its summons more loudly is drumming,
15 While the clang of the village church bell fills the evening entire,
And with longing for you like a faggot my soul is on fire.

O, soon will the village be silent and scarce a light burning,
O, soon·eager steps to the hillside again 'Ill be turning,
And all the night long I will clasp you in love's hungry fashion,
20 And in secret we'll tell to each other the tale of our passion.

196

Till at last we will fall fast asleep neath the shade of that willow,
Your lips drawn aside in a smile and your breast for my pillow,
O, to live one such beautiful night all these wonders fulfilling
And barter the rest of existence, who would not be willing?

DELILAH
(Satire V)

The Bible tells of Samson's wife that she deprived him of his power
By cutting off his hair while he did sleep, and that his foes that hour
Quick fell upon him, bound him hand and foot, and branded out his
eyes,
Which shows what quality of soul is hid beneath sweet woman's guise.
5 Young men, you, who filled with dreams' enchantment, a woman's
graces would fain,
When glows the moon's bright golden shield o'er field and sylvan lane
And splashes on the earth green shadows that with mystery are fraught,
Remember that a woman's skirts are long, her understanding short.
For you are drunken with the magic of a wondrous summer dream
10 That in *you* is lighted . . . But ask her longing, and I deem
That she will speak to you of frills and bows, and of the latest mode,
While secretly within your heart there beats the rhythm of an ode . . .
So, when she leans upon you fondlingly and fills you with her spells,
Beware 'tis demon lore. Think what the Bible of Delilah tells.

15 She is winsome, it is understood, and childish are her wiles,
Sweet girlish dimples still adorn her cheeks whene'er she smiles,
And there are dimples at the corners of her mouth that murder hides,
And on each finger there are dimples too, and many more besides.
Not too small, and not too portly, not too slight, yet slim of waist,
20 Just an armful for a lover, just designed to be embraced;
All she says seems to become her, all she does befits her too,
All she wears sits well upon her, just as though it were her due.

198

When she speaks her voice is pleasing, even her silence does endear,
Though her words may say "Get from me," will her smile say "No,
come here!"
25 And her stride is smooth as music, music rustles from her dress,
Languorous in every movement, always courting a caress.
Till, when rising on her tiptoes for her lips to reach your own,
She will kiss you with a secret warmth and mystery unknown,
A secret warmth that nowhere else than in a woman's soul can burn.
30 O, ravishing indeed the bliss that you imagine you will learn
When in her circling arms you watch the glow of love her cheeks engage !
She — so queenlike and so wayward; you — more fervent than her page.
You will fancy in your rapture when you gaze into her eyes
You have learned to value living right, and even death appraise.
35 And thus poisoned by a delicate, agreeable dejection,
You will see in her the reigning queen of your sad mind's affection
And fancying for you are shed the tears that on her lashes gleam,
Far more beautiful than Venus Anadyomene she will seem;
Until lost in lote's oblivion, where the hours take swiftest flight,
40 Every day she will grow dearer, more adored every night.

Illusion ! How don't you understand? The expression of her gentle face
Is nothing but a mask, a lie; her smile, her sadness, a grimace.
How don't you see to make believe, to cheat is all her heart's concern
And that you give your very sould to her, but get naught in return.
45 Vain indeed the seven-stringed lyre, true companion of your wooing,
Sings unheard with sombre cadence the complaint of your undoing.
O'er your eyes a veil of fable with deft fingers she has lain
As when the frosty flowers of winter spread their wonder o'er the pane,
While in your heart still summer blows; until you cry "Dear love
allow
50 My flowing tears to bless with pious bitter reverence your brow !"
How should she guess it is a demon in your heart that does pursue
Her charm with such strange thirsty fire; a demon in your heart,
not *you;*
And that this demon laughing, weeping tears unable to restrain

Would but capture her in order that he might himself explain.
55 Like a struggling armless sculptor in his torment does he seem,
Or a composer deaf becoming at the moment all supreme
When at last he hears the music of the planets on their courses
Born of cosmic gravity and flying centrifugal forces.
Little does she guess that demon is but for his model wooing;
60 Marble she with eyes of shadow and a voice like pigeons cooing.
Nor does he require that she upon a sacrificial altar die,
As was the sacred ritual custom once in ages long gone by
When a virgin for the model of a goddess had been chosen
And her graceful living loveliness in deathless marble frozen.

65 But to understand himself this demon would from death arise,
Ravished by the fire within him, thus himself to recognize;
Painting then his longing ardour and his passion's thirsty flow
In divine adonic verses, as did Horace long ago.
He would draw from vision's wonder many a leaping woodland stream,
70 Humid, shady forest dingle, stars that in the distance gleam,
Until that strange and secret moment of the birth of fairy rhymes
When in his dreams is recreated fairest dream of ancient times.
While with passion deep unbridled he will gaze on her adoring
And within her eyes so childish, sweet salvation there imploring.
75 In his arms would he embrace her while the endless ages rolled,
Melt beneath his burning kisses eyes that shine a radiance cold;
For indeed with so much loving melt at last would heart of stone,
When before her humbly kneeling he entreats in humble tone.
Happiness his soul consuming, he grows mad beneath love's thrill,
80 Midst the tempest of his passion, that grows ever wilder still.
Does she guess a single moment she could give the world entire
Should she let the waves engulf her and content his heart's aspire,
She could flood with starry wonder depths of nameless solitude?

With a smile of courtesan, but with timid eyes and prude,
85 She pretends to understand him. Women all soon flattered are

And will be so long as beauty blows upon this rolling star.
A woman among flowers, a flower among a thousand women is she
And will please to endless time. But let her take a choice of three
Who standing round all tell her that they love her true, and she,
so naive,

90   All of a sudden, you behold, becomes most strangely positive.
She may take for a screen your spirit and heart
Behind which she lures a young suitor, attractive and smart,
Who walks in like an actor, with light steps,
Floating in a wave of spicy fragrance and of chats,
95   Staring at her through his glasses, a pink in his buttonhole,
He is in clothing and in spirit a perfectly tailored work;
All the four kings of the cards may do for her game
And so their place in her heart's pantry is the same . . .
When does my lady gently flirt with eyes both innocent and coy,
100   Dividing up her favours 'twixt an aged rake and unfledged boy,
Her heart does not deceive her, nor subtle understanding cheat
To mix the knave of spades or diamonds with a knave out of the
street
Before your wild demonic longing she will like a hermit speak,
But when appears the knave of spades the youthful blood mounts
to her cheeks
105   And soon her frosty shining eyes his sombre heart with fire accost,
And you will see her sitting there, one leg upon the other crossed,
The weak in wisdom are instead sometimes beautiful forsooth . . .

The dream that strong, outspoken fact or any manifested truth.
Has power upon this world to change the trend of things in any wise,
110   This is the time-old stumbling-block that in the path of progress lies.

And so young man, when filled with dreams' enchantment you a
woman's graces would fain,
When glows the moon's bright golden shield o'er field and sylvan lane
And splashes on the earth green shadows that with mystery are traught,

201

Remember that a woman's skirt is long, her understanding short.
115 For you are drunken with the magic of a wondrous summer dream
That in *you* is lighted...
                              But ask her of her longing, and I deem
That she will speak to you of frills and bows, and of the latest mode,
While secretly within your heart there beats the rhythm of an ode...
120 When you see a stone unfeeling, which for pity has no care,
Pause if there's a demon in you, 'tis Delilah, so take care!

YOU NEVER KNEW MY SOUL

For me in all existence nowhere such wealth abides
As in the tender secret your gentle beauty hides;
For on what other wonder than that of your sweet charm
Would I a lifetime squander of meditation calm
5 On legends and on musing, and thus a language mould
That it with fleeting cadence your loveliness enfold
With chains of flowing images, and on it dreams bestow
That it ne'er till time's ending shall to the darkness go?

Today when all my being to your being is bound,
10 When hid in every sorrow for me a joy is found;
When you to me more lovely than marble do appear
And in your eye is kindled a ray of starlight clear
That while I gaze upon you I feel I must go blind
With so much shining wonder that floods upon my mind;
15 Today when is my longing so tender and so true
As is the very charm itself that does your form endue,
And stronger is the yearning that our two hearts have known
Than light that yearns for darkness, the chisel for the stone;
When my desire is boundless, so gentle and so high
20 As on the earth is nowhere, and nowhere in the sky;
When everything about you for me is magic spell,
A smile, a word, a gesture, no matter ill or well;
When you are the enigma of life for me the whole,
Your words now show me plainly you never knew my soul.

TO THE STAR

So far it is athwart the blue
To where yon star appears,
That for its light to reach our view.
Has needed thousand years.

5   Maybe that ages gone it shed
Its glow, then languished in the skies,
Yet only now its rays have sped
Their journey to our eyes.

The icon of the star that died
10   Slowly the vault ascended;
Time was ere it could first be spied,
We see now what is ended.

So is it when our love's aspire
Is hid beneath night's bowl,
15   The gleam of its extinguished fire
Enkindles yet our soul.

KAMADEVA

With the balm of lover's torment
Dreaming thus my soul to heal,
I, to Kama, God of India,
Kamadeva, did appeal.

5 And he came, the child imperious,
Riding on a cockatoo,
With a winning smile capricious
On his lips of coral hue.

Wings he had, and in his quiver
10 For his arrow did he keep
Naught but scented poison flowers
From the Ganges wide and deep.

Setting in his bow an arrow,
At my breast he aim did take,
15 And since then for ever weeping
Do I lie the nights awake.

Thus it was a poisoned flower
Deep within my breast did send
India's child of purple heavens
20 And illusions without end.

WHY DON'T YOU COME?

See the swallows quit the eaves
And fall the yellow walnut leaves,
The vines with autumn frost are numb,
Why don't you come, why don't you come?

5   Oh, come into my arms' embrace
That I may gaze upon your face,
And lay my head in grateful rest
Against your breast, against your breast!

Do you remember when we strayed
10   The meadows and the secret glade,
I kissed you midst flowering thyme
How many a time, how many a time?

Some women on the earth there are
Whose eyes shine as the evening star,
15   But be their charm no matter what,
Like you they're not, like you they're not!

For you shine in my soul always
More softly than the starlight blaze,
More splendid than the risen sun,
20   Beloved one, beloved one!

206

But it is late in autumn now,
The leaves have fallen from the bough,
The fields are bare, the birds are dumb...
Why don't you come, why don't you come?

CORNELIU M. POPESCU

Născut în București, România, la 16 mai 1958.

Încetează din viață tragic și foarte tînăr, împreună cu mama sa, în cutremurul catastrofal de la 4 martie 1977.

Laureat post-mortem al premiului Academiei Române pentru lucrarea « MIHAI EMINESCU, » Poems, publicată în 1978 de Editura Eminescu.

Aprecieri asupra lucrării:

« . . . dacă în poezie geniile sînt rare (și toți cei care au putut realmente să cunoască poezia lui Eminescu sînt de acord că acesta e un geniu), nu știu dacă a existat vreodată un geniu al traducerii înaintea acestui tînăr român » — Romanian Review » no. 8, 1978.

« Un înzestrat tălmăcitor din Eminescu » — « Tribuna României » no. 141, 15 septembrie 1978.

« Corneliu M. Popescu sau arta traducerii » — « Steaua » no. 1, 1979

« Un traducător de geniu al lui Eminescu: Corneliu M. Popescu » — « Revista Noastră » no. 58—59—60, 1979

« Un nou Eminescu în Engleză » « Secolul 20 » no. 251—252, 11—12, 1981.

Aprecieri similare în: « Contemporanul », « Synthesis », « Cahiers roumains d'études littéraires », « Cronica », « Vatra », « Manuscriptum », « New Muses », Federația Asociațiilor Internaționale de Poezie, Washington, Gazetta di Chieti » Italia, « Darwen Advertister » Anglia, « Tribune », Londra etc.

Fiind considerată o lucrare care sprijină dezvoltarea culturală între națiuni, « the Poetry Society at National Poetry Centre in London », instituie în mai 1983 « the European Poetry Translation Prize in memory of Corneliu M. Popescu ». Din 1987 premiul se acordă în Asociație cu « British Council ».

Mihail Popescu

CORNELIU M. POPESCU

Born in Bucharest, Roumania, on May 16, 1958.

Passed away tragically and very young together with his mother in the catastrophic earthquake of March 4, 1977.

He was awarded the post-mortem prize of the Roumanian Academy for the work "MIHAI EMINESCU, Poems", published in 1978 by the Eminescu Publishing House.

Critical assessments on the work:

" ...while geniuses of poetry are few and far between (and all those who have been able to know Eminescu agree that he was one) we are not aware of any genius of translation before this young Roumanian" — "Romanian Review" no. 8, 1978.

"A gifted interpreter of Eminescu" — "Tribuna României" no. 141, 15 Septembrie 1978.

"Corneliu M. Popescu or the art of translation" — "Steaua" no. 1/1979.

"A genius translator of Eminescu" Corneliu M. Popescu" — "Revista Noastră" no. 58—59—60/1979.

"A New Eminescu in English" — "Secolul 20" — no. 251—252/11—12/1981

Similar appreciation in "Contemporanul", "Synthesis", Cahiers roumains d'études littéraires", "Cronica", "Vatra", "Manuscriptum", "New uses", Federation of International Poetry Associations, Washington, "Gazetta di Chieti", Italia, "Darwen Advertister", England, "Tribune", London, etc.

Being considered a work which strengthens the cultural ties between the nation, the Poetry Society at National Poetry Centre in London initiated in May 1983 "The European Poetry Translation Prize in memory of Corneliu M. Popescu". Since 1987 the prize has been awarded in Association with the British Council.

Mihail Popescu

SUMMARY

Lector Mircea Ciobanu.
Tehnoredactor Constanța Vulcănescu.
Bun de tipar 4 I. Apărut 1989.
Format 16×70×100. Coli tipo 13,5.